Cicero on Social Media

Cicero on Social Media

What the great thinkers of the past
say about the problems of the present

Mike May, EDITOR

ISBN: 978-0-578-37467-3

to:
Hope
Elijah
Zechariah
Joseph

CONTENTS

PREFACE

"test everything that is said and hold on to what is good"
Paul the Apostle, AD c.5-c.67

While it may seem that our generation faces new and unique problems, despite many changes in technology and circumstances, humanity itself has changed little. For many of today's problems, some remarkably similar situations have been met and overcome in the past.

This book offers a cross-section of relevant quotations recounting how some of the greatest thinkers of the past addressed problems comparable to those of the present. Of course these thoughts should not be considered a prescription - things have and will change, and what worked before may not work again. But if we fail to recognize what has been learned in the past, we force ourselves as a society to relearn these lessons at potentially great cost and suffering. Rather, we should start with the assumption that what has worked well in the past is the best place to start looking for what works now.

Other than occasional bracketed text to clarify some context not apparent in the quote, little effort has been made to interpret the text - wherever possible the authors speak for themselves. In some cases, when the relevance of the quotation to the subject may not be clear at first reading, footnotes have been added to draw the reader's attention to the perspective of interest.

Let this book be a short reminder to learn from those who have come before us, to test everything that is said, and to hold on to what is good.

1 ON SOCIAL MEDIA AND FRIENDSHIP

But most people unreasonably, not to speak of modesty, want such a friend as they are unable to be themselves, and expect from their friends what they do not themselves give. The fair course is first to be good yourself, and then to look out for another of like character.

Cicero, 106–43 BC

When, then, a friend meets with an opportunity of depositing a secret in the breast of another, he, in his turn, seeks to share in the same pleasure. He is entreated, to be sure, to say nothing to anybody; and such a condition, if taken in the strict sense of the words, would immediately cut short the chain of these gratifications: but general practice has determined that it only forbids the entrusting of a secret to everybody but one equally confidential friend, imposing upon him, of course, the same conditions. Thus, from confidential friend to confidential friend, the secret threads its way along this immense chain, until, at last, it reaches the ear of him or them whom the first speaker exactly intended it should never reach. However, it would, generally, have to be a long time on the way, if everybody had but two friends, the one who tells him, and the one to whom he repeats it with the injunction of silence. But some highly favoured men there are who reckon these blessings by the hundred, and when the secret comes into the hands of one of these, the circles multiply so rapidly that it is no longer possible to pursue them.

Alessandro Manzoni, 1785–1873

Hippolytus: Two things I know on earth: God's worship first; next, to wind friends about me, few, that thirst to hold them clean of all unrighteousness.

Euripides, 480 or 485–406 BC

Nothing is more disgraceful than a wolfish friendship. Avoid this most of all.

Marcus Aurelius Antoninus, AD 121–180

If a man has frequent business with others, either in the way of conversation, entertainment, or simple familiarity, he must either become like them, or change them to his own fashion. A live coal placed next a dead one will either kindle that or be quenched by it. Such being the risk, it is well to be cautious in admitting intimacies of this sort, remembering that one cannot rub shoulders with a soot-stained man without sharing the soot oneself. What will you do, supposing the talk turns on gladiators, or horses, or prize-fighters, or (what is worse) on persons, condemning this and that, approving the other?

Epictetus, AD c.50–c.138

We must therefore impress upon good men that, should they become inevitably involved in friendships with men of this kind, they ought not to consider themselves under any obligation to stand by friends who are disloyal to the republic.

Cicero, 106–43 BC

But one thing is most admirable (wherewith I will conclude this first fruit of friendship), which is, that this communicating of a man's self to his friend works two contrary effects; for it doubles joys, and cuts griefs in halves. For there is no man that imparts his joys to his friend, but he joys the more; and no man that imparts his griefs to his friend, but he grieves the less.

Francis Bacon, 1561–1626

He that has many friends, has no friends.

Æsop, c.600 BC

It is not in human nature to be indifferent to political power; and if the price men have to pay for it is the sacrifice of friendship, they think their treason will be thrown into the shade by the magnitude of the reward. This is why true friendship is very difficult to find among those who engage in politics and the contest for office. Where can you find the man to prefer his friend's advancement to his own? And to say nothing of that, think how grievous and almost intolerable it is to most men to share political disaster. You will scarcely find any one who can bring himself to do that. And though what Ennius says is quite true,—"the hour of need shows the friend indeed," —yet it is in these two ways that most people betray their untrustworthiness and inconstancy, by looking down on friends when they are themselves prosperous, or deserting them in their distress. A man, then, who has shown a firm, unshaken, and unvarying friendship in both these contingencies we must reckon as one of a class the rarest in the world, and all but superhuman.

Cicero, 106–43 BC

Wouldst thou have men speak good of thee? speak good of them. And when thou hast learned to speak good of them, try to do good unto them, and thus thou wilt reap in return their speaking good of thee.

Epictetus, AD c.50–c.138

In the gymnastic exercises suppose that a man has torn thee with his nails, and by dashing against thy head has inflicted a wound. Well, we neither show any signs of vexation, nor are we offended, nor do we suspect him afterward as a treacherous fellow; and yet we are on our guard against him, not however as an enemy, nor yet with suspicion, but we quietly get out of his way. Something like this let thy behavior be in all the other parts of life; let us overlook many things in those who are like antagonists in the gymnasium. For it is in our power, as I said, to get out of the way, and to have no suspicion nor hatred.

Marcus Aurelius Antoninus, AD 121–180

"My brother ought not to have treated me thus."

True: but he must see to that. However he may treat me, I must deal rightly by him. This is what lies with me, what none can hinder.

Epictetus, AD c.50–c.138

there are a set of malicious, prating, prudent gossips, both male and female, who murder characters to kill time, and will rob a young fellow of his good name before he has years to know the value of it

Richard Brinsley Sheridan, 1751–1816

The practical principle which guides [most people] to their opinions on the regulation of human conduct, is the feeling in each person's mind that everybody should be required to act as he, and those with whom he sympathizes, would like them to act. No one, indeed, acknowledges to himself that his standard of judgement is his own liking; but an opinion on a point of conduct, not supported by reasons, can only count as one person's preference.

John Stuart Mill, 1806–1873

This great gift also Thou bestowed, O my God, my mercy, upon that good handmaid of Thine, in whose womb Thou created me, that between any disagreeing and discordant parties where she was able, she showed herself such a peacemaker, that hearing on both sides most bitter things, such as swelling and indigested choler uses to break out into, when the crudities of enmities are breathed out in sour discourses to a present friend against an absent enemy, she never would disclose aught of the one unto the other, but what might tend to their reconcilement. A small good this might appear to me, did I not to my grief know numberless persons, who through some horrible and wide-spreading contagion of sin, not only disclose to persons mutually angered things said in anger, but add withal things never spoken

Augustine of Hippo, AD 354–430

I meant to say, is she false? Neither more nor less than everyone who has his own objects to attain.

Johann Wolfgang von Goethe, 1749–1832

No change of circumstances can repair a defect of character. We boast our emancipation from many superstitions; but if we have broken any idols, it is through a transfer of the idolatry. What have I gained, that I no longer immolate a bull to Jove, or to Neptune, or a mouse to Hecate; that I do not tremble before the Eumenides, or the Catholic Purgatory, or the Calvinistic Judgment-day,—if I quake at opinion, the public opinion, as we call it; or at the threat of assault, or contumely, or bad neighbors, or poverty, or mutilation, or at the rumor of revolution, or of murder? If I quake, what matters it what I quake at?

Ralph Waldo Emerson, 1803–1882

2 ON FITNESS, DIET, AND HABIT

try thy skill in the sports, if haply thou art practised in any; and thou art like to have knowledge of games, for there is no greater glory for a man while yet he lives, than that which he achieves by hand and foot.

Homer, fl. 850 BC

He took a reasonable care of his body's health, not as one who was greatly attached to life, nor out of regard to personal appearance, nor yet in a careless way, but so that, through his own attention, he very seldom stood in need of the physician's art or of medicine or external applications

Marcus Aurelius Antoninus, AD 121–180

And thus I have done with what concerns the body and health, which reduces itself to these few and easy observable rules: plenty of open air, exercise, and sleep, plain diet, no wine or strong drink, and very little or no physick[1], not too warm and strait clothing, especially the head and feet kept cold, and the feet often us'd to cold water, and expos'd to wet.

John Locke, 1632–1704

---

[1] medication

According to the general regulation, the [miner] is not allowed to halt for breath, except the mine is six hundred feet deep. The average load is considered as rather more than 200 pounds, and I have been assured that one of 300 pounds (twenty-two stone and a half) by way of a trial has been brought up from the deepest mine! At this time the [miners] were bringing up the usual load twelve times in the day; that is 2400 pounds from eighty yards deep; and they were employed in the intervals in breaking and picking ore. These men, excepting from accidents, are healthy, and appear cheerful. Their bodies are not very muscular. They rarely eat meat once a week, and never oftener, and then only the hard dry charqui.[2]

Charles Robert Darwin, 1809–1882

The horse, the cat, the bull, nay the ass itself, have generally a higher stature, and always a more robust constitution, more vigour, more strength and courage in their forests than in our houses; they lose half these advantage by becoming domestic animals; it looks as if all our attention to treat them kindly, and to feed them well, served only to bastardize them. It is thus with man himself. In proportion as he becomes sociable and a slave to others, he becomes weak, fearful, mean-spirited, and his soft and effeminate way of living at once completes the enervation of his strength and of his courage.

Jean Jacques Rousseau, 1712–1778

---

[2] even the most extraordinary daily exercise will not result in muscle growth when paired with a low protein diet

And certainly a man of courage who cannot fence at all and therefore will put all upon one thrust and not stand parrying, has the odds against a moderate fencer, especially if he has skill in wrestling. And therefore, if any provision be to be made against such accidents, and a man to prepare his son for duels, I had much rather mine should be a good wrestler than an ordinary fencer

John Locke, 1632–1704

It is the part of a Christian to take care of his own body for the very purpose that, by its soundness and well-being, he may be enabled to labour, and to acquire and preserve property, for the aid of those who are in want, that thus the stronger member may serve the weaker member, and we may be children of God, thoughtful and busy one for another, bearing one another's burdens, and so fulfilling the law of Christ.

Martin Luther, 1483–1546

never to give children any physick for prevention. The observation of what I have already advis'd, will, I suppose, do that better than the ladies' diet-drinks or apothecaries' medicines. Have a great care of tampering that way, lest, instead of preventing, you draw on diseases. Nor even upon every little indisposition is physick to be given, or the physician to be call'd to children, especially if he be a busy man, that will presently fill their windows with gally-pots, and their stomachs with drugs. It is safer to leave them wholly to nature, than to put 'em into the hands of one forward to tamper, or that thinks children are to be cur'd, in ordinary distempers, by any thing but diet, or by a method very little distant from it: it seeming suitable both to my reason and experience, that the tender constitutions of children should have as little done to them as is possible, and as the absolute necessity of the case requires.

John Locke, 1632–1704

And, as it is said of Laomedon, the Orchomenian, that by advice of his physician, he used to run long distances to keep off some disease of his spleen, and by that means having, through labor and exercise, framed the habit of his body, he betook himself to the great garland games, and became one of the best runners at the long race; so it happened to Demosthenes, who, first venturing upon oratory for the recovery of his own private property, by this acquired ability in speaking, and at length, in public business, as it were in the great games, came to have the preeminence of all competitors in the assembly.

Plutarch, AD c.46–c.120

Therefore, since custom is the principal magistrate of man's life, let men by all means endeavor to obtain good customs. Certainly custom is most perfect when it begins in young years: this we call education; which is, in effect, but an early custom. So we see, in languages the tongue is more pliant to all expressions and sounds, the joints are more supple to all feats of activity and motions, in youth than afterwards.

Francis Bacon, 1561–1626

You must know that it is no easy thing for a principle to become a man's own, unless each day he maintain it and hear it maintained, as well as work it out in life.

Epictetus, AD c.50–c.138

My intention being to acquire the habitude of all these virtues, I judged it would be well not to distract my attention by attempting the whole at once, but to fix it on one of them at a time; and, when I should be master of that, then to proceed to another, and so on

Benjamin Franklin, 1706-1790

3 ON SURVIVING ADOLESCENCE

Show those qualities then which are altogether in thy power: sincerity, gravity, endurance of labour, aversion to pleasure, contentment with thy portion and with few things, benevolence, frankness, no love of superfluity, freedom from trifling magnanimity. Dost thou not see how many qualities thou art immediately able to exhibit, in which there is no excuse of natural incapacity and unfitness, and yet thou still remainest voluntarily below the mark? or art thou compelled through being defectively furnished by nature to murmur, and to be stingy, and to flatter, and to find fault with thy poor body, and to try to please men, and to make great display, and to be restless in thy mind? No, by the gods: but thou mightest have been delivered from these things long ago. Only if in truth thou canst be charged with being rather slow and dull of comprehension, thou must exert thyself about this also, not neglecting it nor yet taking pleasure in thy dullness.

Marcus Aurelius Antoninus, AD 121–180

nobody was ever so cunning as to conceal their being so: and when they are once discovered, every body is shy, every body distrustful of crafty men; and all the world forwardly join to oppose and defeat them; whilst the open, fair, wise man has everybody to make way for him, and goes directly to his business.

John Locke, 1632–1704

Give thy thoughts no tongue, nor any impertinent thought his act. Be thou familiar, but by no means vulgar. The friends thou hast, and their adoption tried, grapple them to thy soul with hoops of steel; but do not dull thy palm with entertainment of each new-hatch'd, unfledged comrade. Beware of entrance to a quarrel; but being in, bear't that the opposed may beware of thee. Give every man thine ear, but few thy voice; take each man's censure, but reserve they judgement. Costly thy habit as thy purse can buy, but not express'd in France; rich, not gaudy; for the apparel oft proclaims the man, and they in France of the best rank and station are most select and generous in that. Neither a borrower nor a lender be; for loan oft loses both itself and friend, and borrowing dulls the edge of husbandry. This above all: to thine own self be true, and it must follow, as the night the day, thou canst not then be false to any man.

William Shakespeare, 1564–1616

Reflect that the chief source of all evils to Man, and of baseness and cowardice, is not death, but the fear of death. Against this fear then, I pray you, harden yourself; to this let all your reasonings, your exercises, your reading tend. Then shall you know that thus alone are men set free.

Epictetus, AD c.50–c.138

I do not wish to push my criticism on the state of things around me to that extravagant mark that shall compel me to suicide, or to an absolute isolation from the advantages of civil society. If we suddenly plant our foot, and say, I will neither eat nor drink nor wear nor touch any food or fabric which I do not know to be innocent, or deal with any person whose whole manner of life is not clear and rational, we shall stand still. Whose is so? Not mine; not thine; not his. But I think we must clear ourselves each one by the interrogation, whether we have earned our bread to-day by the hearty contribution of our energies to the common benefit; and we must not cease to tend to the correction of these flagrant wrongs, by laying one stone aright every day.

Ralph Waldo Emerson, 1803–1882

a man who is good for anything ought not to calculate the chance of living or dying; he ought only to consider whether in doing anything he is doing right or wrong—acting the part of a good man or of a bad

Plato, c.427–347 BC

If you follow the suburban fashion in building a sumptuous-looking house for a little money, it will appear to all eyes as a cheap dear house. There is no privacy that cannot be penetrated. No secret can be kept in the civilized world. Society is a masked ball, where every one hides his real character, and reveals it by hiding. If a man wish to conceal anything he carries, those whom he meets know that he conceals somewhat, and usually know what he conceals. Is it otherwise if there be some belief or some purpose he would bury in his breast? 'Tis as hard to hide as fire. He is a strong man who can hold down his opinion. A man cannot utter two or three sentences, without disclosing to intelligent ears precisely where he stands in life and thought, namely, whether in the kingdom of the senses and the understanding, or, in that of ideas and imagination, in the realm of intuitions and duty. People seem not to see that their opinion of the world is also a confession of character. We can only see what we are, and if we misbehave we suspect others. The fame of Shakespeare or of Voltaire, of Thomas à Kempis, or of Bonaparte, characterizes those who give it. As gaslight is found to be the best nocturnal police, so the universe protects itself by pitiless publicity.

Ralph Waldo Emerson, 1803–1882

Even the line of heroes is not utterly extinct. There is still ever some admirable person in plain clothes, standing on the wharf, who jumps in to rescue a drowning man; there is still some absurd inventor of charities; some guide and comforter of runaway slaves; some friend of Poland; some Philhellene; some fanatic who plants shade-trees for the second and third generation, and orchards when he is grown old; some well-concealed piety; some just man happy in an ill-fame; some youth ashamed of the favors of fortune, and impatiently casting them on other shoulders.

Ralph Waldo Emerson, 1803–1882

It is hard to combine and unite these two qualities, the carefulness of one who is affected by circumstances, and the intrepidity of one who heeds them not. But it is not impossible: else were happiness also impossible. We should act as we do in seafaring. "What can I do?"—Choose the master, the crew, the day, the opportunity. Then comes a sudden storm. What matters it to me? my part has been fully done. The matter is in the hands of another—the Master of the ship. The ship is foundering. What then have I to do? I do the only thing that remains to me—to be drowned without fear, without a cry, without upbraiding God, but knowing that what has been born must likewise perish. For I am not Eternity, but a human being —a part of the whole, as an hour is part of the day. I must come like the hour, and like the hour must pass!

Epictetus, AD c.50–c.138

debauchery sinks the courage of men; and when dissoluteness has eaten out the sense of true honor, bravery seldom stays long after it. And I think it impossible to find an instance of any nation, however renown'd for their valor, who ever kept their credit in arms, or made themselves redoubtable amongst their neighbors, after corruption had once broke through and dissolved the restraint of discipline, and vice was grown to such an head, that it durst shew itself barefaced without being out of countenance.

John Locke, 1632–1704

O young man, ask not respecting that which doth not concern thee; but be silent; for in silence is security from error

Thousand and One Nights, c.1300

But for such footmen as thee and I are, let us never desire to meet with an enemy, nor vaunt as if we could do better, when we hear of others that they have been foiled, nor be tickled at the thoughts of our own manhood; for such commonly come by the worst when tried. Witness Peter, of whom I made mention before. He would swagger, ay he would; he would, as his vain mind prompted him to say, do better, and stand more for his Master than all men; but who so foiled and run down by these Villains as he?

John Bunyan, 1628–1688

When a man humbles himself for his defects, he then easily pacifies others and quickly satisfies those that are angered against him

Thomas à Kempis, c.1379-1471

few are the good and few the evil, and that the great majority are in the interval between them

Plato, c.427–347 BC

The world is a good judge of things, for it is in natural ignorance, which is man's true state. The sciences have two extremes which meet. The first is the pure natural ignorance in which all men find themselves at birth. The other extreme is that reached by great intellects, who, having run through all that men can know, find they know nothing, and come back again to that same ignorance from which they set out; but this is a learned ignorance which is conscious of itself. Those between the two, who have departed from natural ignorance and not been able to reach the other, have some smattering of this vain knowledge, and pretend to be wise. These trouble the world, and are bad judges of everything. The people and the wise constitute the world; these despise it, and are despised. They judge badly of everything, and the world judges rightly of them.

Blaise Pascal, 1623–1662

For while everyone well knows himself to be fallible, few think it necessary to take any precautions against their own fallibility, or admit the supposition that any opinion of which they feel very certain, may be one of the examples of the error to which they acknowledge themselves to be liable.

John Stuart Mill, 1806–1873

The Master said: "Yu, shall I teach thee what is understanding? To know what we know, and know what we do not know, that is understanding."

Confucius, 551-478 BC

Such as are thy habitual thoughts, such also will be the character of thy mind; for the soul is dyed by the thoughts.

Marcus Aurelius Antoninus, AD 121–180

Difficulties often appear greater at a distance than when they are searched into with judgement, and distinguished from the vapors and shadows that attend them.

Daniel Defoe, c.1661–1731

If thou workest at that which is before thee, following right reason seriously, vigorously, calmly, without allowing anything else to distract thee, but keeping thy divine part pure, as if thou shouldst be bound to give it back immediately; if thou holdest to this, expecting nothing, fearing nothing, but satisfied with thy present activity according to nature, and with heroic truth in every word and sound which thou utterest, thou wilt live happy. And there is no man who is able to prevent this

Marcus Aurelius Antoninus, AD 121–180

My will the enemy held, and thence had made a chain for me, and bound me. For of a forward will, was a lust made; and a lust served, became custom; and custom not resisted, became necessity. By which links, as it were, joined together (whence I called it a chain) a hard bondage held me enthralled. But that new will which had begun to be in me, freely to serve Thee, and to wish to enjoy Thee, O God, the only assured pleasantness, was not yet able to overcome my former willfulness, strengthened by age. Thus did my two wills, one new, and the other old, one carnal, the other spiritual, struggle within me; and by their discord, undid my soul.

Augustine of Hippo, AD 354–430

[Dido] was warm'd with the graceful appearance of the hero; she smother'd those sparkles out of decency; but conversation blew them up into a flame. Then she was forced to make a confidante of her whom she best might trust, her own sister, who approves the passion, and thereby augments it; then succeeds her public owning it; and, after that, the consummation. Of Venus and Juno, Jupiter and Mercury, I say nothing, for they were all machining work; but, possession having cool'd [Aeneas'] love, as it increased hers, she soon perceived the change, or at least grew suspicious of a change; this suspicion soon turn'd to jealousy, and jealousy to rage; then she disdains and threatens, and again is humble, and entreats, and, nothing availing, despairs, curses, and at last becomes her own executioner.

John Dryden, 1631-1700

But if, on the other hand, he yield to his inclination, immediately he is weighed down by the condemnation of his conscience; for that he hath followed his own desire, and yet in no way attained the peace which he hoped for. For true peace of heart is to be found in resisting passion, not in yielding to it. And therefore there is no peace in the heart of a man who is carnal, nor in him who is given up to the things that are without him, but only in him who is fervent towards God and living the life of the Spirit.

Thomas à Kempis, c.1379-1471

Wherefore did he create passions within us, pleasures round about us, but that these rightly tempered are the very ingredients of virtue? They are not skillful considerers of human things, who imagine to remove sin by removing the matter of sin....Though ye take from a covetous man all his treasure he has yet one jewel left, ye can not bereave him of his covetousness. Banish all objects of lust, shut up all youth into the severest discipline that can be exercised in any hermitage, ye can not make them chaste, that came not thither so; such great care and wisdom is required to the right managing of this point. Suppose we could expel sin by this means; look how much we thus expel of sin, so much we expel of virtue: for the matter of them both is the same; remove that, and ye remove them both alike. This justifies the high providence of God, who though he command us temperance, justice, continence, yet pours out before us even to a profuseness all desirable things, and gives us minds that can wander beyond all limit and satiety.

John Milton, 1608–1674

the amorous passion is only vanquished by shunning it, and that nobody ought to adventure to wrestle with so strong an adversary; for heavenly forces are necessary for him that would confront the violence of that passion

Miguel de Cervantes Saavedra, 1547–1616

But the best romance [novel] becomes dangerous, if, by its excitement, it renders the ordinary course of life uninteresting, and increases the morbid thirst for useless acquaintance with scenes in which we shall never be called upon to act.

John Ruskin, 1819–1900

All things are lawful for me; but not all things are expedient. All things are lawful for me; but I will not be brought under the power of any. Meats for the belly, and the belly for meats: but God shall bring to nought both it and them. But the body is not for fornication, but for the Lord; and the Lord for the body: and God both raised the Lord, and will raise up us through his power. Know ye not that your bodies are members of Christ? shall I then take away the members of Christ, and make them members of a harlot? God forbid. Or know ye not that he that is joined to a harlot is one body? for, The twain, saith he, shall become one flesh. But he that is joined unto the Lord is one spirit. Flee fornication. Every sin that a man does is without the body; but he that commits fornication sins against his own body. Or know ye not that your body is a temple of the Holy Spirit which is in you, which ye have from God? and ye are not your own; for ye were bought with a price: glorify God therefore in your body.

Paul the Apostle, AD c.5-c.67

It is a hard thing to break through a habit, and a yet harder thing to go contrary to our own will. Yet if thou overcome not slight and easy obstacles, how shalt thou overcome greater ones? Withstand thy will at the beginning, and unlearn an evil habit, lest it lead thee little by little into worse difficulties.

Thomas à Kempis, c.1379-1471

To every man who would rise in dignity as a man, be he rich or poor, ignorant or instructed, there is one essential condition, one effort, one purpose, without which not a step can be taken. He must resolutely purpose and labor to free himself from whatever he knows to be wrong in his motives and life. He who habitually allows himself in any known crime or wrongdoing, effectually bars his progress towards a higher intellectual and moral life. On this point every man should deal honestly with himself. If he will not listen to his conscience, rebuking him for violations of plain duty, let him not dream of self elevation. The foundation is wanting. He will build, if at all, in sand.

William Ellery Channing, 1780-1842

He wants to be great, and he sees himself small. He wants to be happy, and he sees himself miserable. He wants to be perfect, and he sees himself full of imperfections. He wants to be the object of love and esteem among men, and he sees that his faults merit only their hatred and contempt. This embarrassment in which he finds himself produces in him the most unrighteous and criminal passion that can be imagined; for he conceives a mortal enmity against that truth which reproves him, and which convinces him of his faults. He would annihilate it, but, unable to destroy it in its essence, he destroys it as far as possible in his own knowledge and in that of others; that is to say, he devotes all his attention to hiding his faults both from others and from himself, and he cannot endure either that others should point them out to him, or that they should see them.

Blaise Pascal, 1623–1662

This above all: to thine own self be true, and it must follow, as the night the day, thou canst not then be false to any man.[3]

William Shakespeare, 1564–1616

---

[3] this quote is included twice in this book. Earlier in this chapter Polonius' entire monolog is included. Here just the last sentence is included as a contrast to the quote by Pascal, above: "he devotes all his attention to hiding his faults both from others and from himself." This editor submits that to be "true to thine own self" is the opposite of "hiding his faults...from himself." So to combine the two quotes and rephrase we might say, "This above all: be true to yourself by not hiding your faults from yourself."

The strength of a man's virtue must not be measured by his efforts, but by his ordinary life.

Blaise Pascal, 1623–1662

Inquiry is Human; Blind Obedience Brutal. Truth never loses by the one, but often suffers by the other.

William Penn, 1644–1718

What I must do is all that concerns me, not what the people think. This rule, equally arduous in actual and in intellectual life, may serve for the whole distinction between greatness and meanness. It is the harder because you will always find those who think they know what is your duty better than you know it. It is easy in the world to live after the world's opinion; it is easy in solitude to live after our own; but the great man is he who in the midst of the crowd keeps with perfect sweetness the independence of solitude.

Ralph Waldo Emerson, 1803–1882

The lives of former generations are a lesson to posterity; that a man may review the remarkable events which have happened to others, and be admonished; and may consider the history of people of preceding ages, and of all that hath befallen them, and be restrained.

Thousand and One Nights, c.1300

Most of us have intervals of tedium or depression when we try to get out of ourselves. Or it may be some stroke of ill-fortune, some sorrow, some moral lapse, some desperate blunder, locks us up within ourselves as in a dungeon. Then biography comes to our rescue, and we forget ourselves in following the career of other men and women who may have passed through similar ordeals.

William Roscoe Thayer, 1859-1923

The amount and range of experience that comes to the ordinary man is of necessity limited. Most of us are tied to a particular locality, move in a society representing only a few of the myriad human types that exist, spend the majority of our waking hours attending to a more or less monotonous series of duties or enjoying a small variety of recreations. In such a life there is often no great range of opportunity; and the most adventurous career touches, after all, but a few points in the infinite complex of existence. But we have our imaginations, and it is to these that the artist appeals. The discriminating reader of fiction can enormously enlarge his experience of life through his acquaintance with the new tracts brought within his vision by the novelist, at second hand, it is true, but the vivid writer can often bring before our mental eyes scenes and persons whom we can realize and understand with a greater thoroughness than those we perceive directly through our senses.

W. A. Neilson, 1869-1946

Ninety-nine in a hundred of what are called educated men are in this condition, even of those who can argue fluently for their opinions. Their conclusion may be true, but it might be false for anything they know: they have never thrown themselves into the mental position of those who think differently from them, and considered what such persons may have to say; and consequently they do not, in any proper sense of the word, know the doctrine which they themselves profess.

John Stuart Mill, 1806–1873

Hence we may discover the reason why no philosopher, who is rational and modest, has ever pretended to assign the ultimate cause of any natural operation, or to show distinctly the action of that power, which produces any single effect in the universe. It is confessed, that the utmost effort of human reason is to reduce the principles, productive of natural phenomena, to a greater simplicity, and to resolve the many particular effects into a few general causes, by means of reasonings from analogy, experience, and observation. But as to the causes of theses general causes, we should in vain attempt their discovery; nor shall we ever be able to satisfy ourselves, by any particular explication of them.

David Hume, 1711–1776

The great chain of causes, which links one to another, even to the throne of God himself, can never be unravelled by any industry of ours. When we go but one step beyond the immediate sensible qualities of things, we go out of our depth. All we do after is but a faint struggle, that shows we are in an element which does not belong to us.

Edmund Burke, 1729–1797

But in fearful natures [suspicions] gain ground too fast. There is nothing makes a man suspect much, more than to know little; and therefore men should remedy suspicion by procuring to know more, and not to keep their suspicions in smother. What would men have? Do they think those they employ and deal with are saints? Do they not think they will have their own ends, and be truer to themselves than to them?

Francis Bacon, 1561–1626

From causes which appear similar we expect similar effects. This is the sum of all our experimental conclusions.

David Hume, 1711–1776

The Indian prince, who refused to believe the first relations concerning the effects of frost, reasoned justly; and it naturally required very strong testimony to engage his assent to facts, that arose from a state of nature, with which he was unacquainted, and which bore so little analogy to those events, of which he had had constant and uniform experience. Though they were not contrary to his experience, they were not conformable to it.... No Indian, it is evident, could have experience that water did not freeze in cold climates. This is placing nature in a situation quite unknown to him; and it is impossible for him to tell à priori what will result from it. It is making a new experiment, the consequence of which is always uncertain. One may sometimes conjecture from analogy what will follow; but still this is but conjecture. And it must be confessed, that, in the present case of freezing, the event follows contrary to the rules of analogy, and is such as a rational Indian would not look for. The operations of cold upon water are not gradual, according to the degrees of cold; but whenever it comes to the freezing point, the water passes in a moment, from the utmost liquidity to perfect hardness. Such an event, therefore, may be denominated extraordinary, and requires a pretty strong testimony, to render it credible to people in a warm climate: But still it is not miraculous, nor contrary to uniform experience of the course of nature in cases where all the circumstances are the same. The inhabitants of Sumatra have always seen water fluid in their own climate, and the freezing of their rivers ought to be deemed a prodigy: But they never saw water in Muscovy during the winter; and therefore they cannot reasonably be positive what would there be the consequence.

David Hume, 1711–1776

Thus we see that from our entrance into the university unto the last degree received is commonly eighteen or twenty years, in which time, if a student has not obtained sufficient learning thereby to serve his own turn and benefit his commonwealth, let him never look by tarrying longer to come by any more. For after this time, and forty years of age, the most part of students do commonly give over their wonted diligence, and live like drone bees on the fat of colleges, withholding better wits from the possession of their places, and yet doing little good in their own vocation and calling. I could rehearse a number (if I listed) of this sort, as well in one university as the other. But this shall suffice instead of a large report, that long continuance in those places is either a sign of lack of friends, or of learning, or of good and upright life, as Bishop Fox sometime noted, who thought it sacrilege for a man to tarry any longer at Oxford than he had a desire to profit.

William Harrison, 1534–1593

4 ON FAITH AND PURPOSE

.

If we would amend the World, we should mend Our selves; and teach our Children to be, not what we are, but what they should be.

William Penn, 1644–1718

neither may anyone yield or retreat or leave his rank, but whether in battle or in a court of law, or in any other place, he must do what his city and his country order him; or he must change their view of what is just

Plato, c.427–347 BC

But, loyalty, truce! we're on dangerous ground;
Who knows how the fashions may alter?
The doctrine, to-day, that is loyalty sound,
To-morrow may bring us a halter!

Robert Burns, 1759 1796

And yet, where Right or Religion gives a Call, [one who remains neutral] must be a Coward or an Hypocrite. In such Cases we should never be backward: nor yet mistaken. When our Right or Religion is in question, then is the fittest time to assert it. Nor must we always be Neutral where our Neighbors are concerned: For tho' Medling is a Fault, Helping is a Duty. We have a Call to do good, as often as we have the Power and Occasion.

William Penn, 1644–1718

Till the death of Francia, the Dictator of Paraguay, these two countries must remain distinct, as if placed on opposite sides of the globe. And when the old bloody-minded tyrant is gone to his long account, Paraguay will be torn by revolutions, violent in proportion to the previous unnatural calm. That country will have to learn, like every other South American state, that a republic cannot succeed till it contains a certain body of men imbued with the principles of justice and honour.

Charles Robert Darwin, 1809–1882

But, indeed, the dictum that truth always triumphs over persecution, is one of those pleasant falsehoods which men repeat after one another till they pass into commonplaces, but which all experience refutes. History teems with instances of truth put down by persecution. If not suppressed forever, it may be thrown back for centuries. To speak only of religious opinions: the Reformation broke out at least twenty times before Luther, and was put down. The real advantage which truth has, consisted in this, that when an opinion is true, it may be extinguished once, twice, or many times, but in the course of ages there will generally be found persons to rediscover it until someone of its reappearances falls on a time when from favorable circumstances it escapes persecution until it has made such head as to withstand all subsequent attempts to suppress it.

John Stuart Mill, 1806–1873

It must be owned that man, in much of his struggle with the world around him, has fought blindly for his own ultimate interests. His contest, successful for the moment, has too often led to sure and sad disaster. Stripping forests from hill and mountain, he has gained his immediate object in the possession of their abundant stores of timber; but he has laid open the slopes to be parched by drought, or swept bare by rain. Countries once rich in beauty, and plenteous in all what was needful for his support, are now burnt and barren, or almost denuded of their soil. Gradually he has been taught, by his own bitter experience, that while his aim still is to subdue the earth, he can attain it, not by setting nature and her laws at defiance, but by enlisting them in his service.

Sir Archibald Geikie, 1835-1924

And don't be offended at my telling you the truth: for the truth is that no man who goes to war with you or any other multitude, honestly struggling against the commission of unrighteousness and wrong in the State, will save his life; he who will really fight for the right, if he would live even for a little while, must have a private station and not a public one.

Plato, c.427–347 BC

But a man must keep an eye on his [mechanical] servants, if he would not have them rule him. Man is a shrewd inventor, and is ever taking the hint of a new machine from his own structure, adapting some secret of his own anatomy in iron, wood, and leather, to some required function in the work of the world. But it is found that the machine unmans the user. What he gains in making cloth, he loses in general power. There should be temperance in making cloth, as well as in eating. A man should not be a silk-worm, nor a nation a tent of caterpillars. The robust rural Saxon degenerates in the mills to the Leicester stockinger, to the imbecile Manchester spinner,—far on the way to be spiders and needles. The incessant repetition of the same hand-work dwarfs the man, robs him of his strength, wit, and versatility, to make a pin-polisher, a buckle-maker, or any other specialty; and presently, in a change of industry, whole towns are sacrificed like ant-hills, when the fashion of shoe-strings supersedes buckles, when cotton takes the place of linen, or railways of turnpikes, or when commons are inclosed by landlords. The society is admonished of the mischief of the division of labor, and that the best political economy is care and culture of men; for, in these crises, all are ruined except such as are proper individuals, capable of thought, and of new choice and the application of their talent to new labor.

Ralph Waldo Emerson, 1803–1882

To trade freely with oppressors without laboring to dissuade them from such unkind treatment, and to seek for gain by such traffic, tends, I believe, to make them more easy respecting their conduct than they would be if the cause of universal righteousness was humbly and firmly attended to by those in general with whom they have commerce; and that complaint of the Lord by his prophet, "They have strengthened the hands of the wicked," hath very often revived in my mind.

John Woolman, 1720–1772

You make me afraid, but whither shall I fly to be safe? If I go back to mine own country, that is prepared for Fire and Brimstone, and I shall certainly perish there. If I can get to the Cœlestial City, I am sure to be in safety there. I must venture: To go back is nothing but death; to go forward is fear of death, and life everlasting beyond it. I will yet go forward.

John Bunyan, 1628–1688

That which is not good for the hive, neither is it good for the bee.

Marcus Aurelius Antoninus, AD 121–180

These facts have always suggested to man the sublime creed, that the world is not the product of manifold power, but of one will, of one mind; and that one mind is everywhere active, in each ray of the star, in each wavelet of the pool; and whatever opposes that will is everywhere balked and baffled, because things are made so, and not otherwise. Good is positive. Evil is merely privative, not absolute: it is like cold, which is the privation of heat. All evil is so much death or nonentity. Benevolence is absolute and real. So much benevolence as a man hath, so much life hath he. For all things proceed out of this same spirit, which is differently named love, justice, temperance, in its different applications, just as the ocean receives different names on the several shores which it washes. All things proceed out of the same spirit, and all things conspire with it. Whilst a man seeks good ends, he is strong by the whole strength of Nature. In so far as he roves from these ends, he bereaves himself of power, of auxiliaries; his being shrinks out of all remote channels, he becomes less and less, a mote, a point, until absolute badness is absolute death.

Ralph Waldo Emerson, 1803–1882

A lowly knowledge of thyself is a surer way to God than the deep searchings of man's learning. Not that learning is to be blamed, nor the taking account of anything that is good; but a good conscience and a holy life is better than all. And because many seek knowledge rather than good living, therefore they go astray, and bear little or no fruit.

Thomas à Kempis, c.1379-1471

We can now end where we started at the beginning, namely, with the conception of a will unconditionally good. That will is absolutely good which cannot be evil, in other words, whose maxim, if made a universal law, could never contradict itself. This principle then is its supreme law: Act always on such a maxim as thou canst at the same time will to be a universal law; this is the sole condition under which a will can never contradict itself; and such an imperative is categorical. Since the validity of the will as a universal law for possible actions is analogous to the universal connexion of the existence of things by general laws, which is the formal notion of nature in general, the categorical imperative can also be expressed thus: Act on maxims which can at the same time have for their object themselves as universal laws of nature. Such then is the formula of an absolutely good will.

Immanuel Kant, 1724-1804

Man is but a reed, the most feeble thing in nature, but he is a thinking reed. The entire universe need not arm itself to crush him. A vapor, a drop of water suffices to kill him. But, if the universe were to crush him, man would still be more noble than that which killed him, because he knows that he dies and the advantage which the universe has over him; the universe knows nothing of this. All our dignity consists then in thought. By it we must elevate ourselves, and not by space and time which we cannot fill. Let us endeavor then to think well; this is the principle of morality.

Blaise Pascal, 1623–1662

This is the end of the matter; all hath been heard: Fear God, and keep his commandments; for this is the whole duty of man. For God will bring every work into judgment, with every hidden thing, whether it be good, or whether it be evil.

Ecclesiastes, c.900 BC

I took a survey of that variety of sects which are scattered over the face of the earth, and who mutually accuse each other of falsehood and error. I asked which of them was right? Every one of them in their turn answered theirs. "I and my partisans only think truly; all the rest are mistaken." But, how do you know that your sect is in the right? "Because God hath declared so." And who tells you that God hath so declared! "My spiritual guide, who knows it well. My pastor tells me to believe so and so, and accordingly I believe it; he assures me that everyone who says to the contrary speaks falsely; and, therefore, I listen to nobody who controverts his doctrine." How, thought I, is not the truth every where the same? Is it possible that what is true with one person can be false with another? If the method taken by him who is in the right, and by him who is in the wrong, be the same, what merit or demerit hath the one more than the other? Their choice is the effect of accident, and to impute it to them is unjust:—it is to reward or punish them for being born in this or that country. To say that the Deity can judge us in this manner is the highest impeachment of his justice.

Jean Jacques Rousseau, 1712–1778

Let us then examine this point, and say, "God is, or He is not." But to which side shall we incline? Reason can decide nothing here. There is an infinite chaos which separates us. A game is being played at the extremity of this infinite distance where heads or tails will turn up. What will you wager? According to...reason, you can defend neither of the propositions. Do not then reprove for error those who have made a choice; for you know nothing about it. "No, but I blame them for having made, not this choice, but a choice; for again both he who chooses heads and he who chooses tails are equally at fault, they are both in the wrong. The true course is not to wager at all." —Yes; but you must wager. It is not optional. You are embarked. Which will you choose then?....Let us weigh the gain and the loss in wagering that God is. Let us estimate these two chances. If you gain, you gain all; if you lose, you lose nothing. Wager then without hesitation that He is.—"That is very fine. Yes, I must wager; but I may perhaps wager too much."—Let us see. Since there is an equal risk of gain and of loss, if you had only to gain two lives, instead of one, you might still wager....But there is an eternity of life and happiness. And this being so, if there were an infinity of chances, of which one only would be for you, you would still be right in wagering one to win two....But there is here an infinity of an infinitely happy life to gain, a chance of gain against a finite number of chances of loss, and what you stake is finite.

Blaise Pascal, 1623–1662

I found no narrowness respecting sects and opinions, but believed that sincere, upright-hearted people, in every society, who truly love God, were accepted of him.

John Woolman, 1720–1772

My Son! I come down from heaven for thy salvation; I took upon Me thy miseries not of necessity, but drawn by love that thou might learn patience and might bear temporal miseries without murmuring. For from the hour of My birth, until My death upon the Cross, I ceased not from bearing of sorrow; I had much lack of temporal things; I oftentimes heard many reproaches against Myself; I gently bore contradictions and hard words; I received ingratitude for benefits, blasphemies for My miracles, rebukes for My doctrine."

Thomas à Kempis, c.1379-1471

God will pardon you, for He is the most merciful of the merciful.

Mohammed, AD 571-632

Men may Tire themselves in a Labyrinth of Search, and talk of God: But if we would know him indeed, it must be from the Impressions we receive of him; and the softer our Hearts are, the deeper and livelier those will be upon us.

William Penn, 1644–1718

Arjuna: Lord! of the men who serve Thee—true in heart—As God revealed; and of the men who serve, Worshipping Thee Unrevealed, Unbodied, far, Which take the better way of faith and life?

Krishna: Whoever serve Me—as I show Myself- Constantly true, in full devotion fixed, These hold I very holy. But who serve— Worshipping Me The One, The Invisible, The Unrevealed, Unnamed, Unthinkable, Uttermost, All-pervading, Highest, Sure—Who thus adore Me, mastering their sense, Of one set mind to all, glad in all good, These blessed souls come unto Me.... But if thy thought Droops from such height; if you are weak to set Body and soul upon Me constantly, Despair not! give Me lower service! seek To read Me, worshipping with steadfast will; And, if thou canst not worship steadfastly, Work for Me, toil in works pleasing to Me! For he that labors right for love of Me Shall finally attain! But, if in this Thy faint heart fails, bring Me thy failure! find Refuge in Me! let fruits of labor go, Renouncing all for Me, with lowliest heart, So shalt thou come; for, though to know is more Than diligence, yet worship better is Than knowing, and renouncing better still Near to renunciation—very near—Dwells Eternal Peace!

The Bhagavad-Gita, c.200 BC

It is time that honor should be awarded on higher principles than have governed the judgment of past ages. Surely the inventor of the press, the discoverer of the compass, the men who have applied the power of steam to machinery, have brought the human race more largely into their debt than the bloody race of conquerors, and even than many beneficent princes.

William Ellery Channing, 1780-1842

Then I said, But Lord, what is believing? And then I saw from that saying, He that cometh to me shall never hunger, and he that believeth on me shall never thirst, that believing and coming was all one; and that he that came, that, is, ran out in his heart and affections after salvation by Christ, he indeed believed in Christ.

John Bunyan, 1628–1688

Never read thou the word that thou mayest appear more learned or wise; but study for the mortification of thy sins, for this will be far more profitable for than thee the knowledge of many difficult questions.

Thomas à Kempis, c.1379-1471

But this is certain, and an opinion commonly received among theologians, that the action by which he now sustains it is the same with that by which he originally created it; so that even although he had from the beginning given it no other form than that of chaos, provided only he had established certain laws of nature, and had lent it his concurrence to enable it to act as it is wont to do, it may be believed, without discredit to the miracle of creation, that, in this way alone, things purely material might, in course of time, have become such as we observe them at present; and their nature is much more easily conceived when they are beheld coming in this manner gradually into existence, than when they are only considered as produced at once in a finished and perfect state.

René Descartes, 1596–1650

he saw that his misfortunes had already debased his heart;—that the shame and contempt to which he had been exposed had depressed his ambition, and that his disappointed pride, converted into indignation, had deduced, from the injustice and cruelty of mankind, the depravity of human nature and the emptiness of virtue. He had observed religion made use of as a mask to self-interest, and its worship as a cloak to hypocrisy. He had seen the terms heaven and hell prostituted in the subtlety of vain disputes; the joys of the one and the pains of the other being annexed to a mere repetition of words. He had observed the sublime and primitive idea of the Divinity disfigured by the fantastical imaginations of men; and, finding that in order to believe in God it was necessary to give up that understanding he hath bestowed on us, he held in the same disdain as well the sacred object of our idle reveries as those idle reveries themselves. Without knowing anything of natural causes, or giving himself any trouble to investigate them, he remained in a condition of the most stupid ignorance, mixed with profound contempt for those who pretended to greater knowledge than his own

Jean Jacques Rousseau, 1712–1778

lastly, with how unshaken an assurance I believed of what parents I was born, which I could not know, had I not believed upon hearsay—considering all this, Thou didst persuade me, that not they who believed Thy Books (which Thou hast established in so great authority among almost all nations), but they who believed them not, were to be blamed; and that they were not to be heard who should say to me, "How knowest thou those Scriptures to have been imparted unto mankind by the Spirit of the one true and most true God?" For this very thing was of all most to be believed, since no contentiousness of blasphemous questionings, of all that multitude which I had read in the self-contradicting philosophers, could wring this belief from me, "That Thou art" whatsoever Thou wert (what I knew not), and "That the government of human things belongs to Thee."

Augustine of Hippo, AD 354–430

of this we may be certain: a Doctor of the Holy Scriptures can be made by none but the Holy Ghost, as Christ says, "They shall all be taught of God" (John vi. 45). Now the Holy Ghost does not consider red caps or brown, or any other pomp, nor whether we are young or old, layman or priest, monk or secular, virgin or married; nay, He once spoke by an ass against the prophet that rode on it. Would to God we were worthy of having such doctors given us, be they laymen or priests, married or unmarried!

Martin Luther, 1483–1546

Fret not thyself because of evil-doers, Neither be thou envious against them that work unrighteousness. For they shall soon be cut down like the grass, And wither as the green herb. Trust in Jehovah, and do good; Dwell in the land, and feed on his faithfulness. Delight thyself also in Jehovah; And he will give thee the desires of thy heart. Commit thy way unto Jehovah; Trust also in him, and he will bring it to pass. And he will make thy righteousness to go forth as the light, And thy justice as the noonday. Rest in Jehovah, and wait patiently for him: Fret not thyself because of him who prospers in his way, Because of the man who brings wicked devices to pass. Cease from anger, and forsake wrath: Fret not thyself, it tends only to evil-doing. For evil-doers shall be cut off; But those that wait for Jehovah, they shall inherit the land. For yet a little while, and the wicked shall not be: Yea, thou shalt diligently consider his place, and he shall not be. But the meek shall inherit the land, And shall delight themselves in the abundance of peace.

The Book of Psalms, c.1000 BC

yet is even such an infirmity, in the infancy of faith, borne by our mother Charity, till the newborn may grow up unto a perfect man, so as not to be carried about with every wind of doctrine. But in him who in such wise presumed to be the teacher, source, guide, chief of all whom he could so persuade, that whoso followed him thought that he followed, not a mere man, but Thy Holy Spirit; who would not judge that so great madness, when once convicted of having taught any thing false, were to be detested and utterly rejected?

Augustine of Hippo, AD 354–430

From seeing the present state, it is impossible not to look forward with high expectations to the future progress of nearly an entire hemisphere. The march of improvement, consequent on the introduction of Christianity throughout the South Sea, probably stands by itself in the records of history.

Charles Robert Darwin, 1809–1882

If I should go out of church whenever I hear a false statement, I could never stay there five minutes. But why come out? The street is as false as the church, and when I get to my house, or to my manners, or to my speech, I have not got away from the lie.

Ralph Waldo Emerson, 1803–1882

Therefore it is a wickedly devised fable—and they cannot quote a single letter to confirm it—that it is for the Pope alone to interpret the Scriptures or to confirm the interpretation of them. They have assumed the authority of their own selves. And though they say that this authority was given to St. Peter when the keys were given to him, it is plain enough that the keys were not given to St. Peter alone, but to the whole community.

Martin Luther, 1483–1546

There are many who attack...both the missionaries, their system, and the effects produced by it. Such reasoners never compare the present state with that of the island only twenty years ago; nor even with that of Europe at this day; but they compare it with the high standard of Gospel perfection. They expect the missionaries to effect that which the Apostles themselves failed to do. Inasmuch as the condition of the people falls short of this high standard, blame is attached to the missionary, instead of credit for that which he has effected. They forget, or will not remember, that human sacrifices, and the power of an idolatrous priesthood—a system of profligacy unparalleled in any other part of the world—infanticide a consequence of that system—bloody wars, where the conquerors spared neither women nor children—that all these have been abolished; and that dishonesty, intemperance, and licentiousness have been greatly reduced by the introduction of Christianity. In a voyager to forget these things is base ingratitude; for should he chance to be at the point of shipwreck on some unknown coast, he will most devoutly pray that the lesson of the missionary may have extended thus far.

Charles Robert Darwin, 1809–1882

It was Newman's staunch belief in what is intuitive and instinctive that made him accept the wisdom of the race as more trustworthy than the reason of the individual. Consequently he believed that Christian truth is preserved not by the reasoning of the individual but by the diversified powers, insight, and feeling which are found in a long-continuing society. For Newman, therefore, the Catholic Church was the articulate voice of the body of Christian believers in the past—"the concrete representative of things invisible."

Frank Wilson Cheney Hersey, 1876-1959

We often hear the teachers of all creeds lamenting the difficulty of keeping up in the minds of believers a lively apprehension of the truth which they nominally recognize, so that it may penetrate the feelings, and acquire a real mastery over the conduct. No such difficulty is complained of while the creed is still fighting for its existence: even the weaker combatants then know and feel what they are fighting for, and the difference between it and other doctrines...But when it has come to be an hereditary creed, and to be received passively, not actively- when the mind is no longer compelled, in the same degree as at first, to exercise its vital powers on the questions which its belief presents to it, there is a progressive tendency to forget all of the belief except the formularies, or to give it a dull and torpid assent, as if accepting it on trust dispensed with the necessity of realizing it in consciousness, or testing it by personal experience; until it almost ceases to connect itself at all with the inner life of the human being. Then are seen the cases, so frequent in this age of the world as almost to form the majority, in which the creed remains as it were outside the mind, encrusting and petrifying it against all other influences addressed to the higher parts of our nature; manifesting its power by not suffering any rest and living conviction to get in, but itself doing nothing for the mind or heart, except standing sentinel over them to keep them vacant.

John Stuart Mill, 1806–1873

If like Theophilus and Timothy, we have been brought up in the Knowledge of the best Things, 't is our Advantage: But neither they nor we lose by trying their Truth; for so we learn their, as well as its intrinsic Worth. Truth never lost Ground by Enquiry, because she is most of all Reasonable.

William Penn, 1644–1718

His doctrine is, that he who eats or eats not, regards a day, or regards it not, may do either to the Lord. How many other things might be tolerated in peace, and left to conscience, had we but charity, and were it not the chief stronghold of our hypocrisy to be ever judging one another. I fear yet this iron yoke of outward conformity hath left a slavish print upon our necks; the ghost of a linen decency yet haunts us. We stumble and are impatient at the least dividing of one visible congregation from another, though it be not in fundamentals; and through our forwardness to suppress, and our backwardness to recover any enthralled piece of truth out of the grip of custom, we care not to keep truth separated from truth, which is the fiercest rent and disunion of all. We do not see that while we still affect by all means a rigid external formality, we may as soon fall again into a gross conforming stupidity, a stark and dead congealment of wood and hay and stubble forced and frozen together, which is more to the sudden degenerating of a church than many sub-dichotomies of petty schisms.

John Milton, 1608–1674

But it is not the minds of heretics that are deteriorated most, by the ban placed on all inquiry which does not end in the orthodox conclusions. The greatest harm done is to those who are not heretics, and who's whole mental development is cramped, and their reason cowed, by the fear of heresy. Who can compute what the world loses in the multitude of promising intellects combined with timid characters, who dare not follow out any bold, vigorous, independent train of thought, lest it should land them in something which would admit of being considered irreligious or immoral?

John Stuart Mill, 1806–1873

He must be a born leader or misleader of men, or must have been sent into the world unfurnished with that modulating and restraining balance-wheel which we call a sense of humor, who in old age, has as strong a confidence in his opinions and in the necessity of bringing the universe into conformity with them as he had in youth. In a world the very condition of whose being is that it should be in perpetual flux, where all seems mirage, and the one abiding thing is the effort to distinguish realities from appearances, the elderly man must be indeed of a singularly tough and valid fiber who is certain that he has any clarified residuum of experience, any assured verdict of reflection, that deserves to be called an opinion, or who, even if he had, feels that he is justified in holding mankind by the button while he is expounding it.

James Russell Lowell, 1819-1891

We should overcome heretics with books, not with fire, as the old Fathers did. If there were any skill in overcoming heretics with fire, the executioner would be the most learned doctor in the world; and there would be no need to study, but he that could get another into his power could burn him.

Martin Luther, 1483–1546

Heroic Action is paralyzed; for what worth now remains unquestionable with him? At the fervid period when his whole nature cries aloud for Action, there is nothing sacred under who's banner he can act; the course and kind and conditions of free Action are all but undiscoverable. Doubt storms in on him through every avenue; inquires of the deepest painfulest sort must be engaged with; and the invincible energy of young years waste itself in skeptical, suicidal cavillings; in passionate "questioning of Destiny," where to no answer will be returned.

Thomas Carlyle, 1795–1881

It is incomprehensible that God should exist, and it is incomprehensible that He should not exist, that the soul should be joined to the body, and that we should have no soul; that the world should be created, and that it should not be created, &c.; that original sin should be, and that it should not be.

Blaise Pascal, 1623–1662

Hence it follows that if there be in the world but one true religion, and if every one is obliged to adopt it under pain of damnation, it is necessary to spend our lives in the study of all religions,—to visit the countries where they have been established, and examine and compare them with each other. No man is exempted from the principal duty of his species, and no one hath a right to confide in the judgment of another. The artisan who lives only by his industry, the husbandman who cannot read, the timid and delicate virgin, the feeble valetudinarian, all must, without exception, study, meditate, dispute, and travel the world over in search of truth. There would no longer be any settled inhabitants in a country, the face of the earth being covered with pilgrims going from place to place, at great trouble and expense, to verify, examine, and compare the several different systems and modes of worship to be met with in different countries. We must in such a case bid adieu to the arts and sciences, to trade, and to all the civil occupations of life. Every other study must give place to that of religion; while the man who should enjoy the greatest share of health and strength, and make the best use of his time and reason for the longest term of years allotted to human life, would, in his extreme old age, be still perplexed and undecided; and it would be indeed wonderful if, after all his researches, he should be able to learn before his death what religion he ought to have believed and practiced during his life. Do you endeavor to mitigate the severity of this method, and place as little confidence as possible in the authority of your fellow men? In so doing, however, you place in them the greatest confidence: for if the son of a Christian does right in adopting, without a scrupulous and impartial examination, the religion of his father, how can the son of a Turk do wrong in adopting in the same manner the religion of Mahomet? I defy all the persecutors in the world to answer this question in a manner satisfactory to any person of common sense.

Jean Jacques Rousseau, 1712–1778

Undoubtedly some men are more gifted than others, and are marked out for more studious lives. But the work of such men is not to do others' thinking for them, but to help them to think more vigorously and effectually. Great minds are to make others great. Their superiority is to be used, not to break the multitude to intellectual vassalage, not to establish over them a spiritual tyranny, but to rouse them from lethargy, and to aid them to judge for themselves. The light and life which spring up in one soul are to be spread far and wide. Of all treasons against humanity, there is no one worse than his who employs great intellectual force to keep down the intellect of his less favored brother.

William Ellery Channing, 1780-1842

It is no small thing to dwell in a religious community or congregation, and to live there without complaint, and therein to remain faithful even unto death. Blessed is he who hath lived a good life in such a body, and brought it to a happy end. If thou wilt stand fast and wilt profit as thou ought, hold thyself as an exile and a pilgrim upon the earth. Thou wilt have to be counted as a fool for Christ, if thou wilt lead a religious life.

Thomas à Kempis, c.1379-1471

The man who left on the memory of those who witnessed his life and conversation, such an impression of his moral grandeur, that eighteen subsequent centuries have done homage to him as the Almighty in person, was ignominiously put to death, as what? As a blasphemer. Men did not merely mistake their benefactor; they mistook him for the exact contrary of what he was, and treated him as that prodigy of impiety, which they themselves are now held to be, for their treatment of him. The feelings with which mankind now regard these lamentable transactions, especially the latter of the two, render them extremely unjust in their judgment of the unhappy actors. These were, to all appearance, not bad men- not worse than men most commonly are, but rather the contrary; men who possessed in a full, or somewhat more than a full measure, the religious, moral, and patriotic feelings of their time and people: the very kind of men who, in all times, our own included, have every chance of passing through life blameless and respected. The high-priest who rent his garments when the words were pronounced, which, according to all the ideas of his country, constituted the blackest guilt, was in all probability quite as sincere in his horror and indignation, as the generality of respectable and pious men now are in the religious and moral sentiments they profess; and most of those who now shudder at his conduct, if they had lived in his time and been born Jews, would have acted precisely as he did.

John Stuart Mill, 1806–1873

Men never do evil so completely and cheerfully as when they do it from religious conviction.

Blaise Pascal, 1623–1662

Therefore when need requires, and the Pope[4] is a cause of offense to Christendom, in these cases whoever can best do so, as a faithful member of the whole body, must do what he can to procure a true free council. This no one can do so well as the temporal authorities, especially since they are fellow-Christians, fellow-priests, sharing one spirit and one power in all things, and since they should exercise the office that they have received from God without hindrance, whenever it is necessary and useful that it should be exercised. Would it not be most unnatural, if a fire were to break out in a city, and every one were to keep still and let it burn on and on, whatever might be burnt, simply because they had not the mayor's authority, or because the fire perchance broke out at the mayor's house? Is not every citizen bound in this case to rouse and call in the rest? How much more should this be done in the spiritual city of Christ, if a fire of offense breaks out, either at the Pope's government or wherever it may! The like happens if an enemy attacks a town. The first to rouse up the rest earns glory and thanks. Why then should not he earn glory that descries the coming of our enemies from hell and rouses and summons all Christians?

Martin Luther, 1483–1546

---

[4] or the leader of any faith or church

5 ON LEADERSHIP, BUSINESS, AND SUCCESS

But if you ask the business man why he is trying so hard to make money, and express some doubt as to its being worth while—well, let the veil be drawn. He may see you "out of hours," but you will scarcely recover his confidence.

Ralph Barton Perry, 1876-1957

[The native Caribbean] man and [European] man differ so much at bottom in point of inclinations and passions, that what constitutes the supreme happiness of the one would reduce the other to despair. The first sighs for nothing but repose and liberty; he desires only to live, and to be exempt from labour; nay, the ataraxy of the most confirmed Stoic falls short of his consummate indifference for every other object. On the contrary, the citizen always in motion, is perpetually sweating and toiling, and racking his brains to find out occupations still more laborious: He continues a drudge to his last minute; nay, he courts death to be able to live, or renounces life to acquire immortality. He cringes to men in power whom he hates, and to rich men whom he despises; he sticks at nothing to have the honour of serving them; he is not ashamed to value himself on his own weakness and the protection they afford him; and proud of his chains, he speaks with disdain of those who have not the honour of being the partner of his bondage. What a spectacle must the painful and envied labours of an European minister of state form in the eyes of a Caribbean! How many cruel deaths would not this indolent savage prefer to such a horrid life, which very often is not even sweetened by the pleasure of doing good?

Jean Jacques Rousseau, 1712–1778

In such manner he won the Egyptians to himself, so that they consented to be his subjects; and his ordering of affairs was this:—In the early morning, and until the time of the filling of the market he did with a good will the business which was brought before him; but after this he passed the time in drinking and in jesting at his boon-companions, and was frivolous and playful. And his friends being troubled at it admonished him in some such words as these: "O king, thou dost not rightly govern thyself in thus letting thyself descend to behavior so trifling; for thou ought rather to have been sitting throughout the day stately upon a stately throne and administering thy business; and so the Egyptians would have been assured that they were ruled by a great man, and thou wouldest have had a better report: but as it is, thou art acting by no means in a kingly fashion." And he answered them thus: "They who have bows stretch them at such time as they wish to use them, and when they have finished using them they loose them again; for if they were stretched tight always they would break, so that the men would not be able to use them when they needed them. So also is the state of man: if he should always be in earnest and not relax himself for sport at the due time, he would either go mad or be struck with stupor before he was aware; and knowing this well, I distribute a portion of the time to each of the two ways of living."

Herodotus, c. 500 - 424 BC

A man is rich in proportion to the number of things which he can afford to let alone

Henry David Thoreau, 1817-1862

Men in great place are thrice servants: servants of the sovereign or state; servants of fame; and servants of business. So as they have no freedom; neither in their persons, nor in their actions, nor in their times. It is a strange desire, to seek power and to loose liberty: or to seek power over others and to lose power over a man's self. The rising unto place is laborious; and by pains men come to greater pains; and it is sometimes base; and by indignities men come to dignities. The standing is slippery, and the regress is either a downfall, or at least an eclipse, which is a melancholy thing.... Certainly great persons had need to borrow other men's opinions, to think themselves happy; for if they judge by their own feeling, they cannot find it; but if they think with themselves what other men think of them, and that other men would fain be as they are, then they are happy as it were by report; when perhaps they find the contrary within. For they are the first that find their own griefs, though they be the last that find their own faults. Certainly men in great fortunes are strangers to themselves, and while they are in the puzzle of business they have no time to tend their health either of body or mind. [It is a sad fate for a man to die too well known to everybody else, and still unknown to himself].

Francis Bacon, 1561–1626

For, no man can write anything, who does not think that what he writes is for the time the history of the world; or do anything well, who does not esteem his work to be of importance. My work may be of none, but I must not think it of none, or I shall not do it with impunity.

Ralph Waldo Emerson, 1803–1882

Suppose the offer were this: you shall die slowly; your blood shall daily grow cold, your flesh petrify, your heart beat at last only as a rusted group of iron valves. Your life shall fade from you, and sink through the earth into the ice of Carina; but, day by day, your body shall be dressed more gaily, and set in higher chariots, and have more orders on its breast, crowns on its head, if you will. Men shall bow before it. Stare and shout round it, crowd after it up and down the streets; build palaces for it, feast with it at their tables' heads all the night long; your soul shall stay enough within it to know what they do, and feel the wight of the golden dress on its shoulders, and the furrow of the crown-edge on the skull; -no more. Would you take the offer, verbally made by the death-angel? Would the meanest among us take it, think you? Yet practically and verily we grasp at it, every one of us, in a measure; many of us grasp at ti in its fullness of horror. Every many accepts it, who desires to advance in life without knowing what life is; who means only that he is to get more horses, and more footmen, and more fortune, and more public honor, and -not more personal soul. He only is advancing in life, who's heart is getting softer, whose blood warmer, whose brain quicker, whose spirit is entering into Living peace. And the men who have this life in them are the true lords or kings of the earth- they, and they only.

John Ruskin, 1819–1900

Fathers that wear rags
 Do make their children blind;
But fathers that bear bags
 Shall see their children kind.
Fortune, that arrant whore,
 Ne'er turns the key to the poor.

William Shakespeare, 1564–1616

Almost five thousand years agone, there were Pilgrims walking to the Cœlestial City, as these two honest persons are; and Beelzebub, Apollyon, and Legion, with their Companions, perceiving by the path that the Pilgrims made, that their way to the City lay through this Town of Vanity, they contrived here to set up a Fair; a Fair wherein should be sold all sorts of Vanity, and that it should last all the year long: therefore at this Fair are all such Merchandize sold, as Houses, Lands, Trades, Places, Honours, Preferments, Titles, Countries, Kingdoms, Lusts, Pleasures, and Delights of all sorts, as Whores, Bawds, Wives, Husbands, Children, Masters, Servants, Lives, Blood, Bodies, Souls, Silver, Gold, Pearls, Precious Stones, and what not

John Bunyan, 1628–1688

Men of Athens, I honor and love you; but I shall obey God rather than you, and while I have life and strength I shall never cease from the practice and teaching of philosophy, exhorting anyone whom I meet after my manner, and convincing him, saying: O my friend, why do you, who are a citizen of the great and mighty and wise city of Athens, care so much about laying up the greatest amount of money and honor and reputation, and so little about wisdom and truth and the greatest improvement of the soul, which you never regard or heed at all?

Plato, c.427–347 BC

But thou, want not! ask not! Find full reward Of doing right in right! Let right deeds be Thy motive, not the fruit which comes from them. And live in action! Labor! Make thine acts Thy piety, casting all self aside, Contemning gain and merit; equable In good or evil: equability Is Yôg, is piety!

The Bhagavad-Gita, c.200 BC

It is important not only to be moving, but to be moving in the right direction; not only to be doing something well, but to be doing something worth while. This is evidently true, but it is easily forgotten. Hence it becomes the duty of philosophy to remind men of it; to persuade men occasionally to reflect on their ends, and reconsider their whole way of life. To have a philosophy of life is to have reasons not only for the means you have selected, but for what you propose to accomplish by them.

Ralph Barton Perry, 1876-1957

Though our character is formed by circumstances, our own desires can do much to shape those circumstances; and that what is really inspiriting and ennobling in the doctrine of free will, is the conviction that we have real power over the formation of our own character; that our will, by influencing some of our circumstances, can modify our future habits or capabilities of willing

John Stuart Mill, 1806–1873

For that is the thing a man is born to, in all epochs. He is born to expend every particle of strength that God Almighty has given him, in doing the work he finds he is fit for; to stand up to it to the last breath of life, and do his best. We are called upon to do that; and the reward we all get, -which we are perfectly sure of, if we have merited it,-is that we have got the work done, or at least that we have tried to do the work. For that is a great blessing in itself; and I should say, there is not very much more reward than that going in this world.

Thomas Carlyle, 1795–1881

Those only are happy who have their minds fixed on some object other than their own happiness; in the happiness of others, on the improvement of mankind, even on some art or pursuit, followed not as a means, but as itself an ideal end. Aiming thus at something else, they find happiness by the way. The enjoyments of life are sufficient to make it a pleasant thing, when they are taken *en passant*, without being made a principal object. Once make them so, and they are immediately felt to be insufficient. They will not bear a scrutinizing examination. Ask yourself whether you are happy, and you cease to be so. The only chance is to treat, not happiness, but some end external to it, as the purpose of life. Let your self-consciousness, your scrutiny, your self-interrogation, exhaust themselves on that; and if otherwise fortunately circumstanced you will inhale happiness with the air you breathe, without dwelling on it or thinking about it, without either forestalling it in imagination, or putting it to flight by fatal questioning.

John Stuart Mill, 1806–1873

When Thor and his companions arrive at Utgard, he is told that "nobody is permitted to remain here, unless he understand some art, and excel in it all other men." The same question is still put to the posterity of Thor. A nation of laborers, every man is trained to some one art or detail, and aims at perfection in that; not content unless he has something in which he thinks he surpasses all other men. He would rather not do anything at all, than not do it well. I suppose no people have such thoroughness;—from the highest to the lowest, every man meaning to be master of his art.

Ralph Waldo Emerson, 1803–1882

Men seek retreats for themselves, houses in the country, seashores, and mountains; and thou too art wont to desire such things very much. But this is altogether a mark of the most common sort of men, for it is in thy power whenever thou shalt choose to retire into thyself. For nowhere, either with more quiet or more freedom from trouble, does a man retire than into his own soul, particularly when he has within him such thoughts that by looking into them he is immediately in perfect tranquillity; and I affirm that tranquillity is nothing else than the good ordering of the mind. Constantly then give to thyself this retreat, and renew thyself

Marcus Aurelius Antoninus, AD 121–180

You will laugh (and you are quite welcome) when I tell you that your old acquaintance is turned sportsman, and has taken three noble boars. "What!" you exclaim, "Pliny!" —Even he. However, I indulged at the same time my beloved inactivity; and, whilst I sat at my nets, you would have found me, not with boar spear or javelin, but pencil and tablet, by my side. I mused and wrote, being determined to return, if with all my hands empty, at least with my memorandums full. Believe me, this way of studying is not to be despised: it is wonderful how the mind is stirred and quickened into activity by brisk bodily exercise. There is something, too, in the solemnity of the venerable woods with which one is surrounded, together with that profound silence which is observed on these occasions, that forcibly disposes the mind to meditation. So for the future, let me advise you, whenever you hunt, to take your tablets along with you, as well as your basket and bottle, for be assured you will find Minerva no less fond of traversing the hills than Diana. Farewell.

Pliny the Younger, AD c.62–c.113

there is no truth more thoroughly established, than that there exists in the economy and course of nature an indissoluble union between virtue and happiness, between duty and advantage, between the genuine maxims of an honest and magnanimous policy, and the solid rewards of public prosperity and felicity

George Washington, 1732 – 1799

The writer wonders what the coachman or the hunter values in riding, in horses, and dogs. It is not superficial qualities. When you talk with him, he holds these at as slight a rate as you. His worship is sympathetic; he has no definitions, but he is commanded in nature, by the living power which he feels to be there present. No imitation, or playing of these things, would content him; he loves the earnest of the northwind, of rain, of stone, and wood, and iron. A beauty not explicable, is dearer than a beauty which we can see to the end of. It is nature the symbol, nature certifying the supernatural, body overflowed by life, which he worships, with coarse, but sincere rites.

Ralph Waldo Emerson, 1803–1882

Not alike are those of the believers who sit at home without harm, and those who are strenuous in God's way with their wealth and their persons. God hath preferred those who are strenuous with their wealth and their persons to those who sit still, by many degrees, and to each hath God promised good, but God hath preferred the strenuous for a mighty hire over those who sit still

Mohammed, AD 571-632

Fielding, though less verbose, is no less explicit. He claims for "Tom Jones" that "to recommend goodness and innocence hath been my sincere endeavor in this history," and that he has "endeavored to laugh mankind out of their favorite follies and vices."[5]

W. A. Neilson, 1869-1946

such is our nature, and so blind are we indeed, that we see no inconvenience before we feel it; and for a present gain we regard not what damage may ensue to our posterity

William Harrison, 1534–1593

Pol: My lord, I will use them according to their desert.

Ham: God's bodykins, man, much better! Use every man after his desert, and who should scape whipping? Use them after your own honor and dignity. The less they deserve, the more merit is in your bounty. Take them in.

William Shakespeare, 1564–1616

---

[5] in the context of leadership this quote should remind the reader to consider the mode of communication. Fielding, with his book *Tom Jones*, took up the grim cause of aristocratic hypocrisy, but chose to use a tone of laughter because he knew the reading public would be more receptive to this mode of communication

Tzu-hsia, when governor of Chu-fu, asked how to rule. The Master said: "Never be in a hurry: shut thine eyes to small gains. Nought done in a hurry is thorough, and an eye for small gains means big things undone."

Confucius, 551-478 BC

Character is centrality, the impossibility of being displaced or overset. A man should give us a sense of mass. Society is frivolous, and shreds its day into scraps, its conversation into ceremonies and escapes. But if I go to see an ingenious man, I shall think myself poorly entertained if he give me nimble pieces of benevolence and etiquette; rather he shall stand stoutly in his place, and let me apprehend, if it were only his resistance; know that I have encountered a new and positive quality;—great refreshment for both of us.

Ralph Waldo Emerson, 1803–1882

Timely resolution, or determination of what a man is to do, is honourable, as being the contempt of small difficulties and dangers. And irresolution, dishonourable, as a sign of too much valuing of little impediments and little advantages; for when a man has weighed things as long as the time permits, and resolves not, the difference of weight is but little, and therefore, if he resolve not, he overvalues little things, which is pusillanimity.

Thomas Hobbes, 1588–1679

He that over-runs his Business, leaves it for him that follows more leisurely to take it up; which has often proved a profitable Harvest to them that never Sow'd. Tis the Advantage that slower Tempers have upon the Men of lively Parts, that tho' they don't lead, they will Follow well, and Glean Clean.

William Penn, 1644–1718

The gains of ordinary trades and vocations are honest; and furthered by two things chiefly: by diligence, and by a good name for good and fair dealing. But the gains of bargains are of a more doubtful nature; when men shall wait upon others' necessity, broke by servants and instruments to draw them on, put off others cunningly that would be better chapmen, and the like practices, which are crafty and naught.

Francis Bacon, 1561–1626

They that are least divided in their Care, always give the best Account of their Business. As therefore thou art always to pursue the present Subject, till thou hast master'd it, so if it fall out that thou hast more Affairs than one upon thy Hand, be sure to prefer that which is of most Moment, and will least wait thy Leisure. He that Judges not well of the Importance of his Affairs, though he may be always Busy, he must make but a small Progress.

William Penn, 1644–1718

He that is faithful in a very little is faithful also in much: and he that is unrighteous in a very little is unrighteous also in much. If therefore ye have not been faithful in the unrighteous mammon, who will commit to your trust the true riches? And if ye have not been faithful in that which is another's, who will give you that which is your own?[6]

Jesus, 5 BC-AD 33

It is sometimes easier to transact business advantageously with a person who presides over many individuals than with only one of those same individuals, who sees but his own motives, feels but his own passions, seeks only his own ends; while the former instantly perceives a hundred relations, contingencies, and interests, a hundred objects to secure or avoid, and can, therefore, be taken on a hundred different sides.

Alessandro Manzoni, 1785–1873

Such in reality is the absurd confidence which almost all men have in their own good fortune, that wherever there is the least probability of success, too great a share of it is apt to go to them of its own accord.

Adam Smith, 1723–1790

---

[6] in the context of business leadership, we might interpret this to include: "if you have not been faithful in fulfilling the duties of your job, who will give you a promotion?"

we may consider that there is in men's aptness to society, a diversity of nature, rising from their diversity of affections, not unlike to that we see in stones brought together for building of an edifice. For as that stone which by the asperity and irregularity of figure takes more room from others than itself fills, and for the hardness cannot be easily made plain, and thereby hindereth the building, is by the builders cast away as unprofitable and troublesome, so also a man that by asperity of nature will strive to retain those things which to himself are superfluous and to others necessary, and for the stubborness of his passions cannot be corrected, is to be left or cast out of society as cumbersome thereunto. For seeing every man, not only by right but also by necessity of nature, is supposed to endeavour all he can to obtain that which is necessary for his conversation, he that shall oppose himself against it for things superfluous is guilty of the war that thereupon is to follow; and therefore doth that which is contrary to the fundamental law of Nature, which commandeth 'to seek peace'. The observers of this law may be called 'sociable'

Thomas Hobbes, 1588–1679

We are puppets, Man in his pride, and Beauty fair in her flower; Do we move ourselves, or are we moved by an unseen hand at a game that pushes us off from the board, and others ever succeed? Ah yet, we cannot be kind to each other here for an hour; we whisper, and hint, and chuckle, and grin at a brother's shame; however we brave it out, we men are a little breed.

Alfred, Lord Tennyson, 1809–1892

Consider further the difference between the first and second owner of property. Every species of property is preyed on by its own enemies, as iron by rust; timber by rot; cloth by moths; provisions by mould, putridity, or vermin; money by thieves; an orchard by insects; a planted field by weeds and the inroad of cattle; a stock of cattle by hunger; a road by rain and frost; a bridge by freshets. And whoever takes any of these things into his possession, takes the charge of defending them from this troop of enemies, or of keeping them in repair. A man who supplies his own want, who builds a raft or a boat to go a-fishing, finds it easy to calk it, or put in a thole-pin, or mend the rudder. What he gets only as fast as he wants for his own ends, does not embarrass him, or take away his sleep with looking after. But when he comes to give all the goods he has year after year collected, in one estate to his son,—house, orchard, plowed land, cattle, bridges, hardware, woodenware, carpets, cloths, provisions, books, money,—and cannot give him the skill and experience which made or collected these, and the method and place they have in his own life, the son finds his hands full,—not to use these things, but to look after them and defend them from their natural enemies. To him they are not means, but masters. Their enemies will not remit; rust, mould, vermin, rain, sun, freshet, fire, all seize their own, fill him with vexation, and he is converted from the owner into a watchman or a watch-dog to this magazine of old and new chattels.

Ralph Waldo Emerson, 1803–1882

hateful to me even as the gates of hell, is that man, who under stress of poverty speaks words of guile

Homer, fl. 850 BC

miners are a peculiar race of men in their habits. Living for weeks together in the most desolate spots, when they descend to the villages on feast-days, there is no excess of extravagance into which they do not run. They sometimes gain a considerable sum, and then, like sailors with prize-money, they try how soon they can contrive to squander it. They drink excessively, buy quantities of clothes, and in a few days return penniless to their miserable abodes, there to work harder than beasts of burden. This thoughtlessness, as with sailors, is evidently the result of a similar manner of life. Their daily food is found them, and they acquire no habits of carefulness: moreover, temptation and the means of yielding to it are placed in their power at the same time. On the other hand, in Cornwall, and some other parts of England, where the system of selling part of the vein is followed, the miners, from being obliged to act and think for themselves, are a singularly intelligent and well-conducted set of men.

Charles Robert Darwin, 1809–1882

Then came the dealers in stocks and funds, who must be eager, at any expense, to change their ideal paper wealth for the more solid substance of land.

Edmund Burke, 1729–1797

…or fall as the stocks did, and ruin half those in the kingdom…rejoice that they had drawn out in time, and left the present generation to be the bubbles…

Jonathan Swift, 1667–1745

Cast thy bread upon the waters; for thou shalt find it after many days. Give a portion to seven, yea, even unto eight; for thou knows not what evil shall be upon the earth. If the clouds be full of rain, they empty themselves upon the earth; and if a tree fall toward the south, or toward the north, in the place where the tree falls, there shall it be. He that observes the wind shall not sow; and he that regards the clouds shall not reap. As thou knows not what is the way of the wind, nor how the bones do grow in the womb of her that is with child; even so thou knows not the work of God who does all. In the morning sow thy seed, and in the evening withhold not thy hand; for thou knows not which shall prosper, whether this or that, or whether they both shall be alike good.

Ecclesiastes, c.900 BC

Lord Burleigh writes to his son, "that one ought never to devote more than two-thirds of his income to the ordinary expenses of life, since the extraordinary will be certain to absorb the other third."

Ralph Waldo Emerson, 1803–1882

Creon: No thing in use by man, for power of ill, can equal money. This lays cities low, this drives men forth from quiet dwelling-place, this warps and changes minds of worthiest stamp, to turn to deeds of baseless, teaching men all shifts of cunning, and to know the guilt of every impious deed.

Sophocles, c.496–406 BC

As those who try to stand in thy way when thou art proceeding according to right reason, will not be able to turn thee aside from thy proper action, so neither let them drive thee from thy benevolent feelings towards them, but be on thy guard equally in both matters, not only in the matter of steady judgment and action, but also in the matter of gentleness towards those who try to hinder or otherwise trouble thee. For this also is a weakness, to be vexed at them, as well as to be diverted from thy course of action and to give way through fear; for both are equally deserters from their post, the man who does it through fear, and the man who is alienated from him who is by nature a kinsman and a friend.

Marcus Aurelius Antoninus, AD 121–180

In the case of any person whose judgement is really deserving of confidence, how has it become so? Because he has kept his mind open to criticism of his opinions and conduct. Because it has been his practice to listen to all that could be said against him; to profit by as much of it as was just, and expound to himself, and upon occasion to others, the fallacy of what was fallacious.

John Stuart Mill, 1806–1873

The gentleman is a man of truth, lord of his own actions, and expressing that lordship in his behavior, not in any manner dependent and servile either on persons, or opinions, or possessions. Beyond this fact of truth and real force, the word denotes good-nature or benevolence; manhood first, and then gentleness. The popular notion certainly adds a condition of ease and fortune; but that is a natural result of personal force and love, that they should possess and dispense the goods of the world. In times of violence, every eminent person must fall in with many opportunities to approve his stoutness and worth; therefore every man's name that emerged at all from the mass in the feudal ages, rattles in our ear like a flourish of trumpets. But personal force never goes out of fashion. That is still paramount today, and, in the moving crowd of good society, the men of valor and reality are known, and rise to their natural place. The competition is transferred from war to politics and trade, but the personal force appears readily enough in these new arenas.

Ralph Waldo Emerson, 1803–1882

'it were better to lose a pennon than two or three hundred knights and squires and put all our country in adventure.' These words refrained sir Henry and his brother, for they would do nothing against counsel.[7]

Jean Froissart, c.1337–c.1410

---

[7] There are two leadership lessons here: 1) it is better to take a small PR loss (lose a pennon) by walking away from a project, than to risk the business by taking on a project too large and complex to succeed; 2) "do nothing against counsel." Even if the leader likes the idea, if the team thinks it's a bad idea, don't do it.

Let them give to reading...some of the hours which they otherwise employ so uselessly...they will perhaps gain something, and at least will not lose much.
Blaise Pascal, 1623–1662

be slow to speak and quick to act
Confucius, 551-478 BC

Self-trust is the essence of heroism. It is the state of the soul at war, and its ultimate objects are the last defiance of falsehood and wrong, and the power to bear all that can be inflicted by evil agents. It speaks the truth and it is just. It is generous, hospitable, temperate, scornful of petty calculations and scornful of being scorned. It persists; it is of an undaunted boldness and of a fortitude not to be wearied out. Its jest is the littleness of common life. That false prudence which dotes on health and wealth is the foil, the butt and merriment of heroism.
Ralph Waldo Emerson, 1803–1882

The universal cause is like a winter torrent: it carries everything along with it. But how worthless are all these poor people who are engaged in matters political, and, as they suppose, are playing the philosopher! All drivelers. Well then, man: do what nature now requires. Set thyself in motion, if it is in thy power, and do not look about thee to see if any one will observe it; nor yet expect Plato's Republic: but be content if the smallest thing goes on well, and consider such an event to be no small matter. For who can change men's opinions?

Marcus Aurelius Antoninus, AD 121–180

[while a member of parliament] I learnt how to obtain the best I could, when I could not obtain everything; instead of being indignant or dispirited because I could not have entirely my own way, to be pleased and encouraged when I could have the smallest part of it; and when even that could not be, to bear with complete equanimity the being overruled altogether. I have found, through life, these acquisitions to be of the greatest possible importance for personal happiness, and they are also a very necessary condition for enabling any one, either as a theorist or as a practical man, to effect the greatest amount of good compatible with his opportunities.

John Stuart Mill, 1806–1873

According to the system of natural liberty, the sovereign has only three duties to attend to; three duties of great importance, indeed, but plain and intelligible to common understandings; first, the duty of protecting the society from the violence and invasion of other independent societies; secondly, the duty of protecting, as far as possible, every member of the society from the injustice or oppression of every other member of it, or the duty of establishing an exact administration of justice; and, thirdly, the duty of erecting and maintaining certain public works and certain public institutions, which it can never be for the interest of any individual, or small number of individuals, to erect and maintain; because the profit could never repay the expense to any individual or small number of individuals, though it may frequently do much more than repay it to a great society.

Adam Smith, 1723–1790

The people know that they need in their representative much more than talent, namely, the power to make his talent trusted. They cannot come at their ends by sending to Congress a learned, acute, and fluent speaker, if he be not one, who, before he was appointed by the people to represent them, was appointed by Almighty God to stand for a fact,—invincibly persuaded of that fact in himself,—so that the most confident and the most violent persons learn that here is resistance on which both impudence and terror are wasted, namely, faith in a fact

Ralph Waldo Emerson, 1803–1882

Those who govern, having much business on their hands, do not generally like to take the trouble of considering and carrying into execution new projects. The best public measures are therefore seldom adopted from previous wisdom, but forc'd by the occasion.

Benjamin Franklin, 1706-1790

A more striking instance never came under my notice of what, I believe, is the experience of those who best know the working classes, that the most essential of all recommendations to their favor is that of complete straightforwardness; it's presence outweighs in their minds very strong objections, while no amount of other qualities will make amends for it's apparent absence.

John Stuart Mill, 1806–1873

It was truly said, "the best counsellors are the dead:" books will speak plain when counsellors blanch. Therefore it is good to be conversant in them, especially the books of such as themselves have been actors upon the stage[8].

Francis Bacon, 1561–1626

---

[8] It is not Bacon's intent to suggest we focus on the writings of stage actors; rather, we should read the books of those who have acted on the stage we play (that is, have been in roles similar to our own). Corporate leaders should read the books written by the most inspiring CEOs, politicians should read the books written by pre-eminent presidents, etc.

6 ON FAMILY, MARRIAGE, AND PARENTING

Be as busy as you please with discourses of civility to your son, such as is his company, such will be his manners.

John Locke, 1632–1704

The pious instructions of my parents were often fresh in my mind, when I happened to be among wicked children, and were of use to me. Having a large family of children, they used frequently, on first-days, after meeting, to set us one after another to read the Holy Scriptures, or some religious books, the rest sitting by without much conversation; I have since often thought it was a good practice. From what I had read and heard, I believed there had been, in past ages, people who walked in uprightness before God in a degree exceeding any that I knew or heard of now living: and the apprehension of there being less steadiness and firmness amongst people in the present age often troubled me while I was a child.

John Woolman, 1720–1772

The weapons with which we have gained our most important victories, which should be handed down as heirlooms from father to son, are not the sword and the lance, but the bush-whack, the turf-cutter, the spade, and the bog-hoe, rusted with the blood of many a meadow, and begrimed with the dust of many a hard-fought field.

Henry David Thoreau, 1817-1862

It seems plain to me, that the principle of all virtue and excellency lies in a power of denying ourselves the satisfaction of our own desires, where reason does not authorize them. This power is to be got and improv'd by custom, made easy and familiar by an early practice. If therefore I might be heard, I would advise, that, contrary to the ordinary way, children should be us'd to submit their desires, and go without their longings, even from their very cradles. The first thing they should learn to know, should be, that they were not to have anything because it pleas'd them, but because it was thought fit for them. If things suitable to their wants were supply'd to them, so that they were never suffer'd to have what they once cry'd for, they would learn to be content without it, would never, with bawling and peevishness, contend for mastery, nor be half so uneasy to themselves and others as they are, because from the first beginning they are not thus handled. If they were never suffer'd to obtain their desire by the impatience they express'd for it, they would no more cry for another thing, than they do for the moon.

John Locke, 1632–1704

Never trouble your self about those faults in [children], which you know age will cure

John Locke, 1632–1704

As it is present in all persons, so it is in every period of life. It is adult already in the infant man. In my dealing with my child, my Latin and Greek, my accomplishments and my money stead me nothing. they are all lost on him: but as much soul as I have, avails. If I am merely willful, he gives me a Rowland for an Oliver, sets his will against mine, one for one, and leaves me, if I please, the degradation of beating him by my superiority of strength. But if I renounce my will and act for the soul, setting that up as umpire between us two, out of his young eyes looks the same soul; he reveres and loves with me.

Ralph Waldo Emerson, 1803–1882

A certain friend of mine lately chastised his son, in my presence, for being somewhat too expensive in the matter of dogs and horses. "And pray," I asked him, when the youth had left us, "did you never commit a fault yourself which deserved your father's correction? Did you never? I repeat. Nay, are you not sometimes even now guilty of errors which your son, were he in your place, might with equal gravity reprove? Are not all mankind subject to indiscretions? And have we not each of us our particular follies in which we fondly indulge ourselves?" The great affection I have for you induced me to set this instance of unreasonable severity before you—a caution not to treat your son with too much harshness and severity. Consider, he is but a boy, and that there was a time when you were so too. In exerting, therefore, the authority of a father, remember always that you are a man, and the parent of a man.

Pliny the Younger, AD c.62–c.113

The great mistake I have observed in people's [raising] their children, has been, that this has not been taken care enough of in its due season: that the mind has not been made obedient to discipline, and pliant to reason, when at first it was most tender, most easy to be bow'd. Parents being wisely ordain'd by nature to love their children, are very apt, if reason watch not that natural affection very warily, are apt, I say, to let it run into fondness. They love their little ones and it is their duty; but they often, with them, cherish their faults too. They must not be cross'd, forsooth; they must be permitted to have their wills in all things; and they being in their infancies not capable of great vices, their parents think they may safe enough indulge their irregularities, and make themselves sport with that pretty perverseness which they think well enough becomes that innocent age. But to a fond parent, that would not have his child corrected for a perverse trick, but excused it, saying it was a small matter, Solon very well reply'd, aye, but custom is a great one. The fondling must be taught to strike and call names, must have what he cries for, and do what he pleases. Thus parents, by humoring and cockering them when little, corrupt the principles of nature in their children, and wonder afterwards to taste the bitter waters, when they themselves have poison'd the fountain. For when their children are grown up, and these ill habits with them; when they are now too big to be dandled, and their parents can no longer make use of them as play-things, then they complain that the brats are untoward and perverse; then they are offended to see them willful, and are troubled with those ill humors which they themselves infused and fomented in them; and then, perhaps too late, would be glad to get out those weeds which their own hands have planted, and which now have taken too deep root to be easily extirpated.

John Locke, 1632–1704

If severity carry'd to the highest pitch does prevail, and works a cure upon the present unruly distemper, it often brings in the room of it a worse and more dangerous disease, by breaking the mind; and then, in the place of a disorderly young fellow, you have a low spirited moped creature, who, however with his unnatural sobriety he may please silly people, who commend tame inactive children, because they make no noise, nor give them any trouble; yet at last, will probably prove as uncomfortable a thing to his friends, as he will be all his life an useless thing to himself and others.

John Locke, 1632–1704

What it is to know, and not to know (which ought to be the scope of study), what valor, what temperance, and what justice is: what difference there is between ambition and avarice, bondage and freedom, subjection and liberty, by which marks a man may distinguish true and perfect contentment, and how far-forth one ought to fear or apprehend death, grief, or shame.

Michel Eyquem de Montaigne, 1533-1592

I was put to school to get learning, in which I, poor wretch, knew not what use there was; and yet, if idle in learning, I was beaten. For this was judged right by our forefathers; and many, passing the same course before us, framed for us weary paths, through which we were fain to pass; multiplying toil and grief upon the sons of Adam.

Augustine of Hippo, AD 354–430

There is a degree of low stupidity which deprives the soul as it were of life; the voice of conscience is also but little heard by those who think of nothing but the means of subsistence. To rescue this unfortunate youth from the moral death that so nearly threatened him, he began, therefore, by awakening his self-love and exciting in him a due regard for himself. He represented to his imagination a more happy success, from the future employment of his talents; he inspired him with a generous ardor by a recital of the commendable actions of others, and by raising his admiration of those who performed them. In order to detach him insensibly from an idle and vagabond life, he employed him in copying books; and under pretence of having occasion for such extracts, cherished in him the noble sentiment of gratitude for his benefactor. By this method he also instructed him indirectly by the books he employed him to copy; and induced him to entertain so good an opinion of himself as to think he was not absolutely good for nothing, and to hold himself not quite so despicable in his own esteem as he had formerly done.

Jean Jacques Rousseau, 1712–1778

Virtue is harder to be got than a knowledge of the world; and if lost in a young man, is seldom recover'd. Sheepishness and ignorance of the world, the faults imputed to a private education, are neither the necessary consequences of being [educated] at home, nor if they were, are they incurable evils. Vice is the more stubborn, as well as the more dangerous evil of the two; and therefore in the first place to be fenced against.

John Locke, 1632–1704

But this gamesome humor, which is wisely adapted by nature to their age and temper, should rather be encouraged to keep up their spirits, and improve their strength and health, than curb'd and restrain'd; and the chief art is to make all that they have to do, sport and play too.

John Locke, 1632–1704

It is, no doubt, a very laudable effort, in modern teaching, to render as much as possible of what the young are required to learn, easy and interesting to them. But when this principle is pushed to the length of not requiring them to learn anything but what has been made easy and interesting, one of the chef objects of education is sacrificed. I rejoice in the decline of the old brutal and tyrannical system of teaching, which, however, did succeed in enforcing habits of application; but the new, as it seems to me, is training up a race of men who will be incapable of doing anything which is disagreeable to them.

John Stuart Mill, 1806–1873

It is simple error to insist that a traditional range of studies—the classics, science, mathematics, even history, or English—provide the only possible culture for freedom. Schools must meet the need of the world as frankly and directly as they can, without squeamish prejudice against practical or vocational studies. Shop-work may afford more liberal culture to a given boy than Greek—and the problem of educational values is always thus specific. The only profitable distinction between liberal studies and vocational studies is one which looks out and forward to the life the individual is to lead. A man's calling, if it be of much difficulty, demands vocational training; his life in the family, the community, the state, and the church demands an education which may justly be called liberal; the worthy use of his leisure demands an education which may properly be called cultural. But what is vocational for the artist will be cultural for others; and a given subject may serve many uses in every normal life. A complete education will prepare for life in all its relationships, either by direct study of the problems they present, or by the study of subjects valuable in one of them or in all.

Henry Wyman Holmes, 1880-1960

To conclude this part, which concerns a young gentleman's studies, his tutor should remember, that his business is not so much to teach him all that is knowable, as to raise in him a love and esteem of knowledge; and to put him in the right way of knowing and improving himself when he has a mind to it.

John Locke, 1632–1704

It never was wealth, it never was wealth,
 that bought contentment, peace, or pleasure;
the bands and bliss of mutual love,
O that's the chiefest world's treasure.
Robert Burns, 1759-1796

Yet it is in these dear intimacies, beyond all others, that we must strive and do battle for the truth. Let but a doubt arise, and alas! All the previous intimacy and confidence is but another charge against the person doubted.
Robert Louis Balfour Stevenson, 1850–1894

Marry with a woman thine equal
Pittacus, c.640 – 568 BC

My sisters sat with me and the young man; and, in their conversation with me, said, O our sister, what dost thou purpose to do with this handsome youth? I answered, I desire to take him as my husband:—and, turning to him, and approaching him, I said, O, my master, I wish to make a proposal to thee, and do not thou oppose it. He replied, I hear and obey
Thousand and One Nights, c.1300

And may the gods grant thee all thy heart's desire: a husband and a home, and a mind at one with his may they give—a good gift, for there is nothing mightier and nobler than when man and wife are of one heart and mind in a house, a grief to their foes, and to their friends great joy, but their own hearts know it best.'

Homer, fl. 850 BC

Give a man a horse he can ride,
 Give a man a boat he can sail;
And his rank and wealth, his straight and health
 on sea nor shore shall fail.
Give a man a pipe he can smoke,
 give a man a book he can read;
And his home is bright with a calm delight,
 though the room be poor indeed.
Give a man a girl he can love,
 as I, O my love, love thee;
And his heart is great with the pulse of Fate,
 at home, on land, on sea.

James Thomson, 1834–1882

7 ON POLITICS, POLITICIANS, AND POLICY

All silencing of discussion is an assumption of infallibility.
John Stuart Mill, 1806–1873

I well know with what atrocious insinuations your ears have been filled by them, in order to render our cause most odious in your esteem; but your clemency should lead you to consider that, if accusation be accounted a sufficient evidence of guilt, there will be an end of all innocence in words and actions.
John Calvin, 1509-1564

Silence is the greatest persecution; the saints were never silent. It is true that a call is necessary; but it is not from the decrees of the Council that we must learn whether we are called, it is from the necessity of speaking. Now, after Rome has spoken, and we think that she has condemned the truth, and that they have written it, and after the books which have said the contrary are censured; we must cry out so much the louder, the more unjustly we are censured, and the more violently they would stifle speech, until there come a Pope who hears both parties, and who consults antiquity to do justice. So the good Popes will find the Church still in outcry.
Blaise Pascal, 1623–1662

And it is not difficult to show, by abundant instances, that to extend the bounds of what may be called moral police, until it encroaches on the most unquestionably legitimate liberty of the individual, is one of the most universal of all human propensities.

John Stuart Mill, 1806–1873

There is yet behind of what I purposed to lay open, the incredible loss, and detriment that this plot of licensing puts us to, more than if some enemy at sea should stop up all our havens and ports, and creeks, it hinders and retards the importation of our richest merchandise, truth; nay it was first established and put into practice by anti-christian malice and mystery on set purpose to extinguish, if it were possible, the light of Reformation, and to settle falsehood; little differing from that policy wherewith the Turk upholds his Koran, by the prohibition of printing.

John Milton, 1608–1674

In self-trust all the virtues are comprehended. Free should the scholar be,—free and brave. Free even to the definition of freedom, "without any hindrance that does not arise out of his own constitution." Brave; for fear is a thing which a scholar by his very function puts behind him.

Ralph Waldo Emerson, 1803–1882

I will give no deadly medicine to any one if asked, nor suggest any such counsel; and in like manner I will not give to a woman a pessary to produce abortion.

Hippocrates, c. 460–c. 370 BC

And slay not your children for fear of poverty; we will provide for them; beware! for to slay them is ever a great sin!

Mohammed, AD 571-632

A traveller has no protection besides his firearms; and the constant habit of carrying them is the main check to more frequent robberies.

Charles Robert Darwin, 1809–1882

a Republic trusting to her own forces, is with greater difficulty than one which relies on foreign arms brought to yield obedience to a single citizen. Rome and Sparta remained for ages armed and free. The Swiss are at once the best armed and the freest people in the world.

Niccolo Machiavelli, 1469–1527

the most embarrassing of all conditions in those times, was that of an animal, without claws, and without teeth, which yet, nevertheless, had no inclination to be devoured
Alessandro Manzoni, 1785–1873

Along the side of the Chaucians and Cattans dwell the Cheruscans; a people who finding no enemy to rouse them, were enfeebled by a peace over lasting and uniform, but such as they failed not to nourish. A conduct which proved more pleasing than secure; since treacherous is that repose which you enjoy amongst neighbours that are very powerful and very fond of rule and mastership. When recourse is once had to the sword, modesty and fair dealing will be vainly pleaded by the weaker; names these which are always assumed by the stronger. Thus the Cheruscans, they who formerly bore the character of good and upright, are now called cowards and fools; and the fortune of the Cattans who subdued them, grew immediately to be wisdom.
Tacitus, AD c.54-c.117

Yea this thing they chiefly reprove among other nations, that innumerable books of laws and expositions upon the same be not sufficient. But they think it against all right and justice that men should be bound to those laws, which either be in number more than be able to be read, or else blinder and darker, than that any man can well understand them.
Sir Thomas More, 1478-1535

[death] is too extreme and cruel a punishment for theft, and yet not sufficient to refrain men from theft. For simple theft is not so great an offense, that it ought to be punished with death. Neither there is any punishment so horrible, that it can keep them from stealing, which have no other craft, whereby to get their living. Therefore in this point, not you only, but also the most part of the world, be like evil schoolmasters, which be readier to beat, than to teach their scholars. For great and horrible punishments be appointed for thieves, whereas much rather provision should have been made, that there were some means, whereby they might get their living, so that no man should be driven to this extreme necessity, first to steal, and then to die.

Sir Thomas More, 1478-1535

Ignorance of the causes and original constitution of right, equity, law, and justice, disposeth a man to make custom and example the rule of his actions; in such manner as to think that unjust which it hath been the custom to punish, and that just of the impunity and approbation whereof they can produce an example, or, as the lawyers which only use this false measure of justice barbarously call it, a precedent; like little children, that have no other rule of good and evil manners but the correction they receive from their parents and masters; save that children are constant to their rule, whereas men are not so; because, grown strong and stubborn, they appeal from custom to reason, and from reason to custom, as it serves their turn

Thomas Hobbes, 1588–1679

For this is not the liberty which we can hope, that no grievance ever should arise in the commonwealth, that let no man in this world expect; but when complaints are freely heard, deeply considered, and speedily reformed, then is the utmost bound of civil liberty attained, that wise men look for.

John Milton, 1608–1674

Chorus: Yea, for of choice he did his mother slay.
Athena: Urged by no fear of other wrath and doom?
Chorus: What spur can rightly goad to matricide?
Athena: Two stand to plead—one only have I heard.
Chorus: He will not swear nor challenge us to oath.
Athena: The form of justice, not its deed, thou wills.[9]

Aeschylus, 525–456 BC

When a person, either by express promise or by conduct, has encouraged another to rely upon his continuing to act in a certain way-to build expectations and calculations, and stake any part of his plan of life upon that supposition, a new series of moral obligations arises on his part towards that person, which may possibly be overruled, but can not be ignored.

John Stuart Mill, 1806–1873

---

[9] Aeschylus notes that, even with extreme crimes such as matricide, you must hear both sides of the story to find justice. If you refuse to hear both sides you may arrive at the appearance of justice (form of justice) but not actual justice (not its deed).

It considers every taxpayer as much in duty bound to support ultimate social improvement through education as to direct social improvement through public enterprises of any other sort. Personal return cannot be taken into the account; the good to be achieved is primarily a public good, in which the childless also share. And the problems of education are problems of public policy, involving the whole theory of the state, of government, of the social order, and of civic progress.

Henry Wyman Holmes, 1880-1960

An education established and controlled by the State, should only exist, if it exist at all, as one among many competing experiments, carried on for the purpose of example and stimulus, to keep the others up to a certain standard of excellence.

John Stuart Mill, 1806–1873

But there are more than you ever heard of who die of grief in this island of ours. I will tell you a common case. The rules of Eton require that a boy on the foundation should be there twelve years: he is superannuated at eighteen, consequently he must come at six. Children torn away from mothers and sisters at that age not infrequently die. I speak of what I know. The complaint is not entered by the registrar as grief; but that it is.

Thomas De Quincey, 1785–1859

The instrument for enforcing the [education] law could be no other than public examinations, extending to all children, and beginning at an early age.

John Stuart Mill, 1806–1873

The most unhappy of all men is the man who cannot tell what he is going to do, who has got no work cut-out for him in the world, and does not go into it. For work is the grand cure of all the maladies and miseries that ever beset mankind, -honest work, which you intend getting done.

Thomas Carlyle, 1795–1881

Commerce and manufactures can seldom flourish long in any state which does not enjoy a regular administration of justice, in which the people do not feel themselves secure in the possession of their property, in which the faith of contracts is not supported by law, and in which the authority of the state is not supposed to be regularly employed in enforcing the payment of debts from all those who are able to pay. Commerce and manufactures, in short, can seldom flourish in any state in which there is not a certain degree of confidence in the justice of government.

Adam Smith, 1723–1790

But when the price of food reaches a certain point, there always arises (at least, hitherto it has always arisen; and if it is so still, after all that has been written by so many learned men, what must it have been in those days!)—there always arises an opinion among the many that it is not the effect of scarcity. They forget that they had foreseen and predicted such an issue; they suddenly fancy that there is plenty of corn, and that the evil proceeds from there not being as much distributed as is required for consumption; propositions sufficiently preposterous, but which flatter both their anger and their hopes. Corn monopolists, either real or imaginary, large landholders, the bakers who purchased corn, all, in short, who had either little or much, or were thought to have any, were charged with being the causes of the scarcity and dearness of provisions; they were the objects of universal complaint, and of the hatred of the multitude of every rank....The magistrates, therefore, busied themselves in fixing the highest price that was to be charged upon every commodity; in threatening punishment to any one who should refuse to sell; and making other regulations of a similar nature. As, however, all human precautions, how vigorous soever, can neither diminish the necessity of food, nor produce crops out of season: and as these individual precautions offered no very inviting terms to other countries where there might be a superabundance, the evil continued and increased. The multitude attributed such an effect to the scarcity and feebleness of the remedies, and loudly solicited some more spirited and decisive measures.

Alessandro Manzoni, 1785–1873

It was Amasis too who established the law that every year each one of the Egyptians should declare to the ruler of his district, from what source he got his livelihood, and if any man did not do this or did not make declaration of an honest way of living, he should be punished with death. Now Solon the Athenian received from Egypt this law and had it enacted for the Athenians, and they have continued to observe it, since it is a law with which none can find fault.

Herodotus, c.500 - 424 BC

When, by different taxes upon the necessaries and conveniences of life, the owners and employers of capital stock find, that whatever revenue they derive from it, will not, in a particular country, purchase the same quantity of those necessaries and conveniences which an equal revenue would in almost any other, they will be disposed to remove to some other. And when, in order to raise those taxes, all or the greater part of merchants and manufacturers, that is, all or the greater part of the employers of great capitals, come to be continually exposed to the mortifying and vexatious visits of the tax-gatherers, this disposition to remove will soon be changed into an actual removal. The industry of the country will necessarily fall with the removal of the capital which supported it, and the ruin of trade and manufacturers will follow the declension of agriculture.

Adam Smith, 1723–1790

Then, again, do not tell me, as a good man did today, of my obligation to put all poor men in good situations. Are they my poor? I tell thee, thou foolish philanthropist, that I grudge the dollar, the dime, the cent I give to such men as do not belong to me and to whom I do not belong. There is a class of persons to whom by all spiritual affinity I am bought and sold; for them I will go to prison if need be; but your miscellaneous popular charities; the education at college of fools; the building of meeting-houses to the vain end to which many now stand; alms to sots, and the thousand-fold Relief Societies;—though I confess with shame I sometimes succumb and give the dollar, it is a wicked dollar, which by-and-by I shall have the manhood to withhold.

Ralph Waldo Emerson, 1803–1882

High taxes, sometimes by diminishing the consumption of the taxed commodities, and sometimes by encouraging smuggling, frequently afford a smaller revenue to government than what might be drawn from more moderate taxes.

Adam Smith, 1723–1790

State Socialism would cut off the very roots in personal character- self-help, forethought, and frugality - which nourish and sustain the trunk and branches of every vigorous Commonwealth.

James Russell Lowell, 1819-1891

I hope we shall never be so totally lost to all sense of the duties imposed upon us by the law of social union, as upon any pretext of public service, to confiscate the goods of a single unoffending citizen. Who but a tyrant (a name expressive of everything which can vitiate and degrade human nature) could think of seizing on the property of men, unaccused, unheard, untried, by whole descriptions, by hundreds and thousands together?

Edmund Burke, 1729–1797

For it was well and truly said that the first destroyer of the liberties of a people is he who first gave them bounties and largesses. At Rome the mischief seems to have stolen secretly in, and by little and little, not being at once discerned and taken notice of.

Plutarch, AD c.46–c.120

Aristides said "When I discharged my office well and faithfully," said he, "I was insulted and abused; but now that I have allowed the public thieves in a variety of malpractices, I am considered an admirable patriot. I am more ashamed, therefore, of this present honor than of the former sentence; and I commiserate your condition, with whom it is more praiseworthy to oblige ill men than to conserve the revenue of the public."

Plutarch, AD c.46–c.120

Familiar was each face, and dear as life, That went unto the war, but thither, whence a warrior went of old, doth nought return – only a spear and sword, and ashes in an urn! For Ares, lord of strife, who doth the swaying scales of battle hold, war's money-changer, giving dust for gold, sends back, to hearts that held them dear, scant ash of warriors, wept with many a tear, light to the hand, but heavy to the soul; yea, fills the light urn full with what survived the flame – death's dusty measure of a hero's frame!

Aeschylus, 525–456 BC

The English are not fired with the splendid folly of making conquests, but would only prevent their neighbours from conquering. They are not only jealous of their own liberty, but even of that of other nations. The English were exasperated against Louis XIV. for no other reason but because he was ambitious, and declared war against him merely out of levity, not from any interested motives.

Voltaire, 1694–1778

The Romans, therefore, foreseeing evils while they were yet far off, always provided against them, and never suffered them to take their course for the sake of avoiding war; since they knew that war is not so to be avoided, but is only postponed to the advantage of the other side. They chose, therefore, to make war with Philip and Antiochus in Greece, that they might not have to make it with them in Italy, although for a while they might have escaped both. This they did not desire, nor did the maxim leave it to Time, which the wise men of our own day have always on their lips, ever recommend itself to them. What they looked to enjoy were the fruits of their own valor and foresight. For Time, driving all things before it, may bring with it evil as well as good.

Niccolo Machiavelli, 1469–1527

They account fortune amongst things slippery and uncertain, but bravery amongst such as are never-failing and secure; and, what is exceeding rare nor ever to be learnt but by a wholesome course of discipline, in the conduct of the general they repose more assurance than in the strength of the army. Their whole forces consist of foot, who besides their arms carry likewise instruments of iron and their provisions. You may see other Germans proceed equipped to battle, but the Cattans so as to conduct a war.

Tacitus, AD c.54-c.117

during the time men live without a common power to keep them all in awe, they are in that condition which is called war, and such a war as is of every man against every man. For 'war' consisteth not in battle only or the act of fighting, but in a tract of time wherein the will to contend by battle is sufficiently known, and therefore the notion of 'time' is to be considered in the nature of war, as it is in the nature of weather. For as the nature of foul weather lieth not in a shower or two of rain but in an inclination thereto of many days together, so the nature of war consisteth not in actual fighting but in the known disposition thereto during all the time there is no assurance to the contrary. All other time is 'peace.'

Thomas Hobbes, 1588–1679

Consider for what you are answerable if you are wrong. For the most fatal war that ever yet desolated a country. Your refusal is the signal that at once summons the provinces to arms, that justifies every cruelty for which Spain has hitherto so anxiously sought a pretext. With a single nod you will excite to the direst confusion what, with patient effort, we have so long keep in abeyance. Think of the towns, the nobles, the people; think of commerce, agriculture, trade! Realize the murder, the desolation! Calmly the soldier beholds his comrade fall beside him in the battlefield. But towards you, carried downwards by the stream, shall float the corpses of citizens, of children, of maidens, till, aghast with horror, you shall no longer know whose cause you are defending, since you shall see those, for whose liberty you drew the sword, perishing around you. And what will be your emotions when conscience whispers, "it was for my own safety that I drew it"?

Johann Wolfgang von Goethe, 1749–1832

We feared that, if we killed one of them, or struck him, or drove him away, they would kill us, on account of their excessive number; for numbers prevail against courage; and we feared them lest they should plunder our goods and our commodities.

Thousand and One Nights, c.1300

Neither is the opinion of some of the Schoolmen to be received, that a war cannot justly be made but upon a precedent injury or provocation. For there is no question but a just fear of an imminent danger, though there be no blow given, is a lawful cause of a war.

Francis Bacon, 1561–1626

I became a soldier from party feeling - I do not myself know on what political principles - and from the whim that it is good for every honorable man to try the profession of arms for a time, to make himself familiar with danger, and to learn coolness and determination.

Gotthold Ephraim Lessing, 1729–1781

As for the wars which were anciently made on the behalf of a kind of party, or tacit conformity of estate, I do not see how they may be well justified: as when the Romans made a war for the liberty of Grecia; or when the Lacedæmonians and Athenians made wars to set up or pull down democracies and oligarchies; or when wars were made by foreigners, under the pretense of justice or protection, to deliver the subjects of others from tyranny and oppression; and the like.

Francis Bacon, 1561–1626

Twas not the welfare of the state, not the honour of the king, not the tranquillity of the provinces, that brought him hither. For his own selfish ends he, the warrior, has counseled war, that in war the value of his services might be enhanced. He has excited this monstrous insurrection that his presence might be deemed necessary in order to quell it.

Johann Wolfgang von Goethe, 1749–1832

"No man," said the Master, "ready to fly unarmed at a tiger, or plunge into a river and die without a pang should be with me; but one, rather, who is wary before a move and gains his end by well-laid plans."

Confucius, 551-478 BC

I am not aware that any community has a right to force another to be civilized. So long as the sufferers by the bad law do not invoke assistance from other communities, I cannot admit that persons entirely unconnected with them ought to step in and require that a condition of things with which all who are directly interested appear to be satisfied, should be put an end to because it is a scandal to persons some thousands of miles distant, who have no part or concern in it.

John Stuart Mill, 1806–1873

May the Gods continue and perpetuate amongst these nations, if not any love for us [Romans], yet by all means this their animosity and hate towards each other: since whilst the destiny of the Empire thus urges it, fortune cannot more signally befriend us, than in sowing strife amongst our foes.

Tacitus, AD c.54-c.117

in all times kings and persons of sovereign authority, because of their independency, are in continual jealousies and in the state and posture of gladiators, having their weapons pointing, and their eyes fixed on one another, that is, their forts, garrisons, and guns, upon the frontiers of their kingdoms, and continual spies upon their neighbours: which is a posture of war

Thomas Hobbes, 1588–1679

a people...the most noble, such as would rather maintain their grandeur by justice than violence. They live in repose, retired from broils abroad, void of avidity to possess more, free from a spirit of domineering over others. They provoke no wars, they ravage no countries, they pursue no plunder. Of their bravery and power, the chief evidence arises from hence, that, without wronging or oppressing others, they are come to be superior to all. Yet they are all ready to arm, and if an exigency require, armies are presently raised, powerful and abounding as they are in men and horses; and even when they are quiet and their weapons laid aside, their credit and name continue equally high.

Tacitus, AD c.54-c.117

the consuls themselves being unwilling to run the hazard of a battle, when the time of their office was almost ready to expire

Plutarch, AD c.46-c.120

For never having reflected in tranquil times that there might come a change (and it is human nature when the sea is calm not to think of storms)

Niccolo Machiavelli, 1469-1527

In popular tumults there is always a certain number of men, who, either from overheated passions, or from fanatical persuasion, or from wicked designs, or from an execrable love of destruction, do all they can to push matters to the worst; they propose or send the most inhuman advice, and fan the flame whenever it seems to be sinking: nothing is ever too much for them, and they wish for nothing so much as that the tumult should have neither limits nor end

Alessandro Manzoni, 1785–1873

Nevertheless, that our free will be not wholly set aside, I think it may be the case that Fortune is the mistress of one half our actions, and yet leaves the control of the other half, or a little less, to ourselves. And I would liken her to one of those wild torrents which, when angry, overflow the plains, sweep away trees and houses, and carry off soil from one bank to throw it down upon the other. Every one flees before them, and yields to their fury without the least power to resist. And yet, though this be their nature, it does not follow that in seasons of fair weather, men cannot, by constructing weirs and moles, take such precautions as will cause them when again in flood to pass off by some artificial channel, or at least prevent their course from being so uncontrolled and destructive. And so it is with Fortune, who displays her might where there is no organized strength to resist her, and directs her onset where she knows that there is neither barrier nor embankment to confine her.

Niccolo Machiavelli, 1469–1527

Such is the melancholy condition of the Russian empire, as is shown in the accounts of those who have had sufficient opportunity of observation. The Czar himself is powerless against the bureaucratic body; he can send any one of them to Siberia, but he cannot govern without them, or against their will. On every decree of his they have a tacit veto, by merely refraining from carrying it into effect. In countries of more advanced civil action and of a more insurrectionary spirit the public, accustomed to expect everything to be done for them by the State, or at least to do nothing for themselves without asking from the State not only leave to do it, but even how it is to be done, naturally hold the State responsible for all evil which befalls them, and when the evil exceeds their amount of patience, they rise against the government and make what is called a revolution; whereupon somebody else, with or without legitimate authority from the nation, vaults into the seat, issues his orders to the bureaucracy, and everything goes on much as it did before; the bureaucracy being unchanged, and nobody else being capable of taking their place.

John Stuart Mill, 1806–1873

And well ordered States and wise Princes have provided with extreme care that the nobility shall not be driven to desperation, and that the commons shall be kept satisfied and contented; for this is one of the most important matters that a Prince has to look to.

Niccolo Machiavelli, 1469–1527

he began to gather that he had come to a city in a state of insurrection, and that this was a day of victory; that is to say, when every one helped himself in proportion to his inclination and power, giving blows in payment

Alessandro Manzoni, 1785–1873

On a review of the circumstances, there were two principal fruits of the insurrection: destruction and actual loss of provision, in the insurrection itself, and a consumption, while the tariff lasted, immense, immeasurable, and, so to say, jovial, which rapidly diminished the small quantity of grain that was to have sufficed till the next harvest.

Alessandro Manzoni, 1785–1873

To tyrants others have their country sold, Imposing foreign lords, for foreign gold; Some have old laws repealed, new statutes made, Not as the people pleased, but as they paid

Virgil, 70-19 BC

There is a troublesome Humor some Men have, that if they may not lead, they will not follow; but had rather a thing were never done, than not done their own way, tho' other ways very desirable.

William Penn, 1644–1718

The man who is ready to give and expecting to receive offense every moment, naturally seeks allies and companions. Hence the tendency of individuals to unite into classes was in these times carried to the greatest excess; new societies were formed, and each man strove to increase the power of his own party to the greatest degree

Alessandro Manzoni, 1785–1873

in our opinion, there is no more unsafe politician than a conscientiously rigid doctrinaire, nothing more sure to end in disaster than a theoretic scheme of policy that admits of no pliability for contingencies. True, there is a popular image of an impossible He, in who's plastic hands the submissive destinies of mankind become as wax, and to whose commanding necessity the toughest facts yield with the graceful pliancy of fiction; but in real life we commonly find that the men who control circumstances, as it is called, are those who have learned to allow for the influence of their eddies, and have the nerve to turn them to account at the happy instant. [President] Lincoln's perilous task has been to carry a rather shaky raft through the rapids, making fast the unrulier logs as he could snatch opportunity, and the country is to be congratulated that he did not think it his duty to run straight at all hazards, but cautiously to assure himself with his setting-pole where the main current was, and keep steadily to that. He is still in wild water, but we have faith that his skill and sureness of eye will bring him out right at last.

James Russell Lowell, 1819-1891

A great amount of time, which, if well used, would form an enlightened population, is now wasted on newspapers and conversations, which inflame the passions, which unscrupulously distort the truth, which denounce moral independence as treachery to one's party, which agitate the country for no higher end than a triumph over opponents; and thus multitudes are degraded into men-worshippers or men-haters, into the dupes of the ambitious, or the slaves of a faction.

William Ellery Channing, 1780-1842

Judge, Sir, of my surprise, when I found that a very great proportion of the [British Parliament] (a majority, I believe, of the members who attended) was composed of practitioners in the law. It was composed, not of distinguished magistrates, who had given pledges to their country of their science, prudence, and integrity; not of leading advocates, the glory of the bar; not of renowned professors in universities;— but for the far greater part, as it must in such a number, of the inferior, unlearned, mechanical, merely instrumental members of the profession. There were distinguished exceptions; but the general composition was of obscure provincial advocates, of stewards of petty local jurisdictions, country attorneys, notaries, and the whole train of the ministers of municipal litigation, the fomenters and conductors of the petty war of village vexation.

Edmund Burke, 1729–1797

Is [the proposed bill] good?—the bad man embraces it, and by the supposition, you reject it. Is it bad?—he vituperates it, and that suffices for driving you into its embrace. You split upon the rocks because he has avoided them; you miss the harbor because he has steered into it! Give yourself up to any such blind antipathy, you are no less in the power of your adversaries than if, by a correspondently irrational sympathy and obsequiousness, you put yourself into the power of your friends.

Sydney Smith, 1771–1845

He is well aware of the low Reckoning the Labors of indifferent Authors are under, at a Time when hardly any Thing passes for current, that is not calculated to flatter the Sharpness of contending Parties

William Penn, 1644–1718

I hear a preacher[10] announce for his text and topic the expediency of one of the institutions of his church. Do I not know beforehand that not possibly can he say a new and spontaneous word? Do I not know that with all this ostentation of examining the grounds of the institution he will do no such thing? Do I not know that he is pledged to himself not to look but at one side, the permitted side, not as a man, but as a parish minister? He is a retained attorney, and these airs of the bench are the emptiest affectation....This conformity makes them not false in a few particulars, authors of a few lies, but false in all particulars. Their every truth is not quite true. Their two is not the real two, their four not the real four: so that every word they say chagrins us and we know not where to begin to set them right. Meantime nature is not slow to equip us in the prison-uniform of the party to which we adhere. We come to wear one cut of face and figure, and acquire by degrees the gentlest asinine expression. There is a mortifying experience in particular, which does not fail to wreak itself also in the general history; I mean "the foolish face of praise," the forced smile which we put on in company where we do not feel at ease, in answer to conversation which does not interest us. The muscles, not spontaneously moved but moved by a low usurping willfulness, grow tight about the outline of the face, and make the most disagreeable sensation; a sensation of rebuke and warning which no brave young man will suffer twice.

Ralph Waldo Emerson, 1803–1882

---

[10] or a politician on the party's policy goals

Observations on my reading history, in Library, May 19th, 1731. "That the great affairs of the world, the wars, revolutions, etc., are carried on and affected by parties. "That the view of these parties is their present general interest, or what they take to be such. "That the different views of these different parties occasion all confusion. "That while a party is carrying on a general design, each man has his particular private interest in view. "That as soon as a party has gain'd its general point, each member becomes intent upon his particular interest; which, thwarting others, breaks that party into divisions, and occasions more confusion. "That few in public affairs act from a mere view of the good of their country, whatever they may pretend; and, tho' their actings bring real good to their country, yet men primarily considered that their own and their country's interest was united, and did not act from a principle of benevolence. "That fewer still, in public affairs, act with a view to the good of mankind.

Benjamin Franklin, 1706-1790

Like other tyrannies, the tyranny of the majority was at first, and is still vulgarly, held in dread, chiefly as operating through the acts of the public authorities. But reflecting persons perceived that when society is itself the tyrant - society collectively, over the separate individuals who compose it - its means of tyrannizing are not restricted to the acts which it may do by the hands of its political functionaries. Society can and does execute it's own mandates; and if it issues wrong mandates instead of right, or any mandates at all in things with which it ought not to meddle, it practices a social tyranny more formidable than many kinds of political oppression, since, though not usually upheld by such extreme penalties, it leaves fewer means of escape, penetrating much more deeply into the details of life, and enslaving the soul itself.

John Stuart Mill, 1806–1873

You can talk a mob into anything; its feelings may be -usually are- on the whole, generous and right; but it has no foundation for them, no hold of them; you may tease or tickle it into any, at your pleasure; it thinks by infection, for the most part, catching an opinion like a cold, and there is nothing so little that it will not roar itself wild about when the fit is on; -nothing so great but it will forget in an hour, when the fit is past.

John Ruskin, 1819–1900

The Secretary, however, says, "I claim, as a citizen, a right to legislate whenever my social rights are invaded by the social act of another." And now for the definition of these "social rights." "If anything invades my social rights, certainly the traffic in strong drink does. It destroys my primary right of security, by constantly creating and stimulating social disorder. It invades my right of equality, by deriving a profit from the creation of a misery, I am taxed to support. It impedes my right of free moral and intellectual development, by surrounding my path with dangers, and by weakening and demoralizing society, from which I have a right to claim mutual aid and intercourse" A theory of "social rights," the like of which probably never before found its way into distinct language-being nothing short of this-that it is the absolute social right of every individual, that every other individual shall act in every respect exactly as he ought; that whosoever fails thereof in the smallest particular, violates my social right, and entitles me to demand from the legislature the removal of the grievance. So monstrous a principle is far more dangerous than any single interference with liberty; there is no violation of liberty which it would not justify; it acknowledges no right to any freedom what ever, except perhaps to that of holding opinions in secret, without ever disclosing them; for the moment an opinion which I consider noxious, passes any one's lips, it invades all the "social rights" attributed to me by the alliance.

John Stuart Mill, 1806–1873

First, then, it was not the plague, absolutely not—by no means: the very utterance of the term was prohibited. Then, it was pestilential fevers: the idea was indirectly admitted in an adjective. Then, it was not the true nor real plague; that is to say, it was the plague, but only in a certain sense; not positively and undoubtedly the plague, but something to which no other name could be affixed. Lastly, it was the plague without doubt, without dispute: but even then another idea was appended to it, the idea of poison and witchcraft, which altered and confounded that conveyed in the word they could no longer repress.

Alessandro Manzoni, 1785–1873

Your words, alas, justify the fears of the people, the universal fear! The king has then resolved as no sovereign ought to resolve. In order to govern his subjects more easily, he would crush, subvert, nay, ruthlessly destroy, their strength, their spirit, and their self-respect! He would violate the inmost core of their individuality, doubtless in view of promoting their happiness. He would annihilate them, that they may assume a new, a different form. Oh! If his purpose be good, he is fatally misguided! It is not the king whom we resist; -we but place ourselves in the way of the monarch, who, unhappily, is about to take the first rash step in a wrong direction.

Johann Wolfgang von Goethe, 1749–1832

Do you imagine that a State can subsist and not be overthrown, in which the decisions of law have no power, but are set aside and overthrown by individuals?

Plato, c.427–347 BC

there were constant apprehensions from robbers within. The sentinels were the worst of all; for, from their office and from having arms in their hands, they robbed with a degree of authority which other men could not imitate.

Charles Robert Darwin, 1809–1882

to prevent the weaker members of the community from being preyed upon by innumerable vultures, it was needful that there should be an animal of prey stronger than the rest, commissioned to keep them down. But as the king of the vultures would be no less bent upon preying upon the flock than any of the minor harpies, it was indispensable to be in perpetual attitude of defense against his beak and claws. The aim, therefore, of patriots, was to set limits to the power which the ruler should be suffered to exercise over the community; and this limitation was what they meant by liberty.

John Stuart Mill, 1806–1873

What is the species of domestic industry which his capital can employ, and of which the produce is likely to be of the greatest value, every individual, it is evident, can, in his local situation, judge much better than any statesman or lawgiver can do for him. The statesman, who should attempt to direct private people in what manner they ought to employ their capitals, would not only load himself with a most unnecessary attention, but assume an authority which could safely be trusted, not only to no single person, but to no council or senate whatever, and which would no-where be so dangerous as in the hands of a man who had folly and presumption enough to fancy himself fit to exercise it.

Adam Smith, 1723–1790

There is, in fact, no recognized principle by which the propriety or impropriety of government interference is customarily tested. People decide according to their personal preferences. Some, wherever they see any good to be done, or evil to be remedied, would willingly instigate the government to undertake the business; while others prefer to bear almost any amount of social evil, rather than add one to the departments of human interests amenable to governmental control.

John Stuart Mill, 1806–1873

If there be any one maxim in politics more certain than another, it is that no possible degree of virtue in the governor can render it expedient for the governed to dispense with good laws and good institutions. Madame De Stael (to her disgrace) said to the Emperor of Russia: "Sire, your character is a constitution for your country, and your conscience its guaranty." His reply was "If that were so, I should be only a happy accident." And this we think one of the truest and most brilliant replies ever made by a monarch.

Sydney Smith, 1771–1845

The establishment of perfect justice, of perfect liberty, and of perfect equality, is the very simple secret which most effectually secures the highest degree of prosperity to all

Adam Smith, 1723–1790

Mankind are greater gainers by suffering each other to live as seems good to themselves, then by compelling each to live as seems good to the rest.

John Stuart Mill, 1806–1873

Aristotle observes, that a democracy has many striking points of resemblance with a tyranny. ""The ethical character is the same; both exercise despotism over the better class of citizens; and decrees are in the one, what ordinances and arrêts are in the other: the demagogue too, and the court favorite, are not infrequently the same identical men, and always bear a close analogy; and these have the principal power, each in their respective forms of government, favorites with the absolute monarch, and demagogues with a people such as I have described." Arist. Politic. lib. iv. cap. 4"

Edmund Burke, 1729–1797

I had an old master once, who possessed a collection of parchments, among which were charters of ancient constitutions, contracts, and privileges. He set great store, too, by the rarest books. One of these contained our whole constitution; how, at first, we Netherlanders had princes of our own, who governed according to hereditary laws, rights, and usages; how our ancestors paid due honour to their sovereign so long as he governed them equitably; and how they were immediately on their guard the moment he was for overstepping his bounds. The states were down upon him at once; for every province, however small, had its own chamber and representatives.

Johann Wolfgang von Goethe, 1749–1832

justice is the maximum of individual self-assertion; it is the function of the state and of the law to make it possible for the individual to act freely. Hence the sphere of law is limited to the minimum of restraint and coercion necessary to allow the maximum of self-assertion by each, limited by the like self-assertion by all

Roscoe Pound, 1870-1964

8 ON DEATH AND AFTERLIFE

As the shades of evening close,
 Beckening thee to long repose;
As life itself becomes disease,
 Seek the chimney-nook of ease;
There ruminate with sober thought,
 On all you've seen, and heard, and wrought,
And teach the sportive younkers round,
 Saws of experience, sage and sound:
Say, man's true, genuine estimate,
 The grand criterion of his fate, Is not,—
Are thou high or low?
 Did thy fortune ebb or flow?
Did many talents gild thy span?
 Or frugal Nature grudge thee one?
Tell them, and press it on their mind,
 As thou thyself must shortly find,
The smile or frown of awful Heaven,
 To virtue or to Vice is giv'n,
Say, to be just, and kind, and wise—
 There solid self-enjoyment lies;
That foolish, selfish, faithless ways
Lead to be wretched, vile, and base.
                    Robert Burns, 1759-1796

Consider, for example, the times of Vespasian. Thou wilt see all these things, people marrying, bringing up children, sick, dying, warring, feasting, trafficking, cultivating the ground, flattering, obstinately arrogant, suspecting, plotting, wishing for some to die, grumbling about the present, loving, heaping up treasure, desiring consulship, kingly power. Well, then, that life of these people no longer exists at all. Again, remove to the times of Trajan. Again, all is the same. Their life, too, is gone. In like manner view also the other epochs of time and of whole nations, and see how many after great efforts soon fell and were resolved into the elements. But chiefly thou should think of those whom thou hast thyself known distracting themselves about idle things, neglecting to do what was in accordance with their proper constitution, and to hold firmly to this and to be content with it. And herein it is necessary to remember that the attention given to everything has its proper value and proportion. For thus thou wilt not be dissatisfied, if thou appliest thyself to smaller matters no further than is fit.

Marcus Aurelius Antoninus, AD 121–180

Happy he, on the weary sea, who hath fled the tempest and won the haven. Happy whoso hath risen, free, above his striving. For strangely graven is the orb of life, that one and another in gold and power may out-pass his brother. And men in their millions float and flow and seethe with a million hopes as leaven; and they win their will, or they miss their will, and the hopes are dead or are pined for still; but whoever can know, as the long days go, that to live is happy, hath found his heaven.

Euripides, 480 or 485–406 BC

The absurdities of yesterday are the common sense of today; the common sense of yesterday is now obsolete and quaint. The crank of the sixteenth century was the man who said that the earth moved; the crank of the twentieth century is the man who says that it does not. Moreover, once common sense is thus reflected upon, it is seen to be in part, at least, the result of wholly irrational forces, such as habit and imitation. What has been long believed, or repeatedly asserted, acquires a hardness and fixity from that fact; in the future it is always easier to believe, more difficult to disbelieve, than anything recent or novel.

Ralph Barton Perry, 1876-1957

Go thy way, eat thy bread with joy, and drink thy wine with a merry heart; for God hath already accepted thy works. Let thy garments be always white; and let not thy head lack oil. Live joyfully with the wife whom thou loves all the days of thy life of vanity, which he hath given thee under the sun, all thy days of vanity: for that is thy portion in life, and in thy labor wherein thou labors under the sun. Whatsoever thy hand finds to do, do it with thy might; for there is no work, nor device, nor knowledge, nor wisdom, in [the grave], whither thou goest.

Ecclesiastes, c.900 BC

Think continually how many physicians are dead after often contracting their eyebrows over the sick; and how many astrologers after predicting with great pretensions the deaths of others; and how many philosophers after endless discourses on death or immortality; how many heroes after killing thousands; and how many tyrants who have used their power over men's lives with terrible insolence as if they were immortal; and how many cities are entirely dead, so to speak, Helice and Pompeii and Herculaneum, and others innumerable. Add to the reckoning all whom thou hast known, one after another. One man after burying another has been laid out dead, and another buries him; and all this in a short time. To conclude, always observe how ephemeral and worthless human things are, and what was yesterday a little mucus, tomorrow will be a mummy or ashes. Pass then through this little space of time conformably to nature, and end thy journey in content, just as an olive falls off when it is ripe, blessing nature who produced it, and thanking the tree on which it grew.

Marcus Aurelius Antoninus, AD 121–180

Better saith he, [who accounts the close of life as one of the benefits of nature]. It is as natural to die as to be born; and to a little infant, perhaps, the one is as painful as the other. He that dies in an earnest pursuit, is like one that is wounded in hot blood; who, for the time, scarce feels the hurt; and therefore a mind fixed and bent upon somewhat that is good doth avert the doles of death. But, above all, believe it, the sweetest canticle is, [Now let thou...depart]; when a man hath obtained worthy ends and expectations.

Francis Bacon, 1561–1626

When attention is concentrated on the scene the thousands of stars on each side of the Milky Way will fill the mind with the consciousness of a stupendous and all-embracing frame, beside which all human affairs sink into insignificance. A new idea will be formed of such a well-known fact of astronomy as the motion of the solar system in space, by reflecting that, during all human history, the sun, carrying the earth with it, has been flying towards a region in or just south of the constellation Lyra, with a speed beyond all that art can produce on earth, without producing any change apparent to ordinary vision in the aspect of the constellation. Not only Lyra and Aquila, but every one of the thousand stars which form the framework of the sky, were seen by our earliest ancestors just as we see them now. Bodily rest may be obtained at any time by ceasing from our labors, and weary systems may find nerve rest at any summer resort; but I know of no way in which complete rest can be obtained for the weary soul—in which the mind can be so entirely relieved of the burden of all human anxiety—as by the contemplation of the spectacle presented by the starry heavens under the conditions just described.

Simon Newcomb, 1835-1909

He was earnest and unwearied in the search of knowledge, with which his vigorous soul is now satisfied, and employed in a continual praise of that God that first breathed it into his active body: that body, which once was a temple of the Holy Ghost, and is now become a small quantity of Christian dust:—

But I shall see it re-animated.

Izaak Walton, 1593–1683

The lingering disorder of a friend of mine gave me occasion lately to reflect that we are never so good as when oppressed with illness. Where is the sick man who is either solicited by avarice or inflamed with lust? At such a season he is neither a slave of love nor the fool of ambition; wealth he utterly disregards, and is content with ever so small a portion of it, as being upon the point of leaving even that little. It is then he recollects there are gods, and that he himself is but a man: no mortal is then the object of his envy, his admiration, or his contempt; and the tales of slander neither raise his attention nor feed his curiosity: his dreams are only of baths and fountains. These are the supreme objects of his cares and wishes, while he resolves, if he should recover, to pass the remainder of his days in ease and tranquillity, that is, to live innocently and happily. I may therefore lay down to you and myself a short rule, which the philosophers have endeavored to inculcate at the expense of many words, and even many volumes; that "we should try and realize in health those resolutions we form in sickness." Farewell

Pliny the Younger, AD c.62–c.113

Thou gave me health to serve thee, and I made a profane use of it. Thou sends me sickness now to correct me; suffer not that I use it to irritate thee by my impatience. I made a bad use of my health, and thou hast justly punished me for it. Suffer not that I make a bad use of my punishment. And since the corruption of my nature is such that it renders thy favors pernicious to me, grant, O my God! that thy all-powerful grace may render thy chastisements salutary. If my heart was full of affection for the world while it retained its vigor, destroy this vigor for my salvation; and render me incapable of enjoying the world, either through weakness of body or through zeal of charity, that I may enjoy but thee alone.

Blaise Pascal, 1623–1662

He that is down needs fear no fall,
  He that is low no pride;
He that is humble, ever shall
  Have God to be his Guide.
I am content with what I have,
  Little be it, or much:
And Lord, contentment still I crave,
  Because thou savest such.
Fulness to such a burden is
  That go on Pilgrimage;
Here little, and hereafter Bliss,
  Is best from age to age.

John Bunyan, 1628–1688

To be, or not to be: that is the question. Whether 'tis nobler in the mind to suffer the slings and arrows of outrageous fortune, or to take arms against a sea of trouble, and by opposing end them. To die; to sleep; no more; and by a sleep to say we end the heart-ache and the thousand natural shocks that flesh is heir to. 'Tis a consummation devoutly to be wish'd. To die; to sleep; - To sleep? Perchance to dream! Aye, there's the rub; for in that sleep of death what dreams may come, when we have shuffled off this mortal coil, must give us pause. There's the respect that makes calamity of so long life. For who would bear the whips and scorns of time, the oppressor's wrong, the proud man's contumely, the pangs of despised love, the law's delay, the insolence of office, and the spurns that patient merit of the unworthy takes, when he himself might his quietus make with a bare bodkin? Who would fardels bear to grunt and sweat under a weary life, but that the dread of something after death, the undiscovered country from whose bourn no traveler returns, puzzles the will and makes us rather bear those ills we have than fly to others that we know not of? Thus conscience does make cowards of us all; and thus the native hue of resolution is sicklied o'er with he pale cast of thought, and enterprises of great pith and moment with this regard their currents turn awry, and lose the name of action.

William Shakespeare, 1564–1616

Child of Adam, let not hope make game of thee. From all that thy hands have reassured thou shalt be removed. I see thee desirous of the world and its embellishments; and the past generations have pursued the same course. They acquired wealth, both lawful and forbidden; but it repelled not fate when the term expired: They led troops in multitudes, and collected riches; and they left their wealth and buildings, and departed to the narrow graves, and lay down in the dust; and there they have remained, pledged for their actions; As if the company of travelers had put down their baggage during night in a house where was no food for guests. And its owner had said to them, O people, there is not any lodging for you in it. So they packed after alighting: And they all thereupon became fearful and timid: neither halting nor journeying was pleasant unto them. Then prepare good provision that will rejoice thee tomorrow; and act not save agreeably with the fear of thy Lord.

Thousand and One Nights, c.1300

This carelessness in a matter which concerns themselves, their eternity, their all, moves me more to anger than pity; it astonishes and shocks me; it is to me monstrous. I do not say this out of the pious zeal of a spiritual devotion. I expect, on the contrary, that we ought to have this feeling from principles of human interest and self-love; for this we need only see what the least enlightened persons see. We do not require great education of the mind to understand that here is no real and lasting satisfaction; that our pleasures are only vanity; that our evils are infinite; and, lastly, that death, which threatens us every moment, must infallibly place us within a few years under the dreadful necessity of being for ever either annihilated or unhappy. There is nothing more real than this, nothing more terrible. Be as heroic as we like, that is the end which awaits the noblest life in the world. Let us reflect on this, and then say whether it is not beyond doubt that there is no good in this life but in the hope of another; that we are happy only in proportion as we draw near it; and that, as there are no more woes for those who have complete assurance of eternity, so there is no more happiness for those who have no insight into it.

Blaise Pascal, 1623–1662

In the corrupted currents of this world offenses' gilded hand may shove by justice, and oft 'tis seen the wicked prize itself buys out the law. But 'tis not so above. There is no shuffling, there the action lies in his true nature; and we ourselves compelled even to the teeth and forehead of our faults, to give in evidence. What then? What rests? Try what repentance can. What can it not? Yet what can it when one cannot repent? O wretched state! O bosom black as death! O limed soul, that, struggling to be free, art more engaged! Help, angles! Make assay! Bow, stubborn knees, and heart with strings of steel, be soft as sinews of the new-born babe! All may be well.

William Shakespeare, 1564–1616

How can it be that the gods, after having arranged all things well and benevolently for mankind, have overlooked this alone, that some men and very good men, and men who, as we may say, have had most communion with the divinity, and through pious acts and religious observances have been most intimate with the divinity, when they have once died should never exist again, but should be completely extinguished? But if this is so, be assured that if it ought to have been otherwise, the gods would have done it. For if it were just, it would also be possible; and if it were according to nature, nature would have had it so. But because it is not so, if in fact it is not so, be thou convinced that it ought not to have been so:—for thou sees even of thyself that in this inquiry thou art disputing with the deity; and we should not thus dispute with the gods, unless they were most excellent and most just;—but if this is so, they would not have allowed anything in the ordering of the universe to be neglected unjustly and irrationally.

Marcus Aurelius Antoninus, AD 121–180

Now it came to pass on one of those days, that he entered into a boat, himself and his disciples; and he said unto them, Let us go over unto the other side of the lake: and they launched forth. But as they sailed he fell asleep: and there came down a storm of wind on the lake; and they were filling with water, and were in jeopardy. And they came to him, and awoke him, saying, Master, master, we perish. And he awoke, and rebuked the wind and the raging of the water: and they ceased, and there was a calm. And he said unto them, Where is your faith? And being afraid they marveled, saying one to another, Who then is this, that he commands even the winds and the water, and they obey him?

Luke the Apostle, fl. AD 60

FURTHER READING

Breadth of reading will keep a man from error's path.
Confucius, 551-478 BC

1. Luke, Acts; The Bible
2. Autobiography, Benjamin Franklin
3. Lives, Plutarch
4. Confessions, Augustine of Hippo
5. Imitation of Christ, Thomas à Kempis
6. Pensées, Pascal
7. Wealth of Nations, Adam Smith
8. On Liberty, John Stuart Mill
9. Federalist Papers; Hamilton, Madison, & Jay
10. On the Revolution in France, Edmund Burke
11. Concerning Education, John Locke
12. Analects, Confucius
13. Meditations, Marcus Aurelius
14. Works, Cicero
15. Origin of Species, Darwin
16. The Prince, Machiavelli
17. Art of War, Sun Tzu
18. Faust, Goethe
19. Essays, Ralph Waldo Emerson
20. Faith of a Savoyard Vicar, Jean-Jacques Rousseau
21. Journal, John Woolman
22. Works, Shakespeare
23. The Betrothed, Manzoni
24. Life of Samuel Johnson, Boswell
25. Iliad & Odyssey, Homer